RESISTING ELEGY

RESISTING ELEGY

ESSAYS ON GRIEF
AND RECOVERY

Joel Peckham

ACADEMY CHICAGO PUBLISHERS

Published in 2011 by
Academy Chicago Publishers
363 West Erie Street
Chicago, Illinois 60654

© 2011 by Joel Peckham

First edition.

Printed and bound in the U.S.A.

Library of Congress Cataloging-in-Publication Data

Peckham, Joel.
Resisting elegy : essays on grief and recovery / Joel Peckham.—1st ed.
p. cm.
Includes bibliographical references and index.
ISBN 978-0-89733-625-3 (alk. paper)
1. Grief. 2. Bereavement—Psychological aspects.
3. Loss (Psychology)
I. Title.
BF575.G7P3784 2011
155.9'37—dc23
2011043521

CONTENTS

Satellites / 9

Scream / 37

The Neverland / 41

Ruins / 75

Resisting Elegy / 107

Please Take What You Want / 121

ACKNOWLEDGEMENTS

Essays from this collection have appeared in *Brevity, Jelly Bucket, The North American Review, South Loop, River Teeth, Under the Sun,* and the anthology *Terror and Transformation* (Wising Up Press).

The way in which a man accepts his fate and all the suffering it entails, the way in which he takes up his cross, gives him ample opportunity—even under the most difficult circumstances—to add a deeper meaning to his life. It may remain brave, dignified, unselfish. Or in the bitter fight for self-preservation, he may forget his human dignity and become no more than an animal.

— VICTOR FRANKL, *MAN'S SEARCH FOR MEANING*[1]

Nothing will shake a man—or at any rate a man like me—out of his merely verbal thinking and his merely notional beliefs. He has to be knocked silly before he comes to his senses. Only torture will bring out the truth. Only under torture does he discover it himself.

— C.S. LEWIS, *A GRIEF OBSERVED*

---

1. Victor Frankl, *Man's Search For Meaning* (Boston: Beacon Press, 2006) 67.

SATELLITES

OCTOBER, 2005

His wife shuffles to his bed.
They part, when the shades are bright,
she sleeps, eyes opened. To stay with him,
he would need to ask the light to shade
its rising, she would need to ask the sun
to let her speak, he would need to ask
her words to shame him quiet.

— "Lovers," Susan Atefat-Peckham

But there are stories that don't have beginnings, I tell my students as I limp toward the whiteboard, marker in hand—ready to attack and dismantle the Freytag triangle—its neat symmetry, its infuriating geometry. I take a deep breath. Where we start is everything, all is exposition, and no truths are as simple as this. So "Tell me a story / In this century and moment of mania, / Tell me a story." But where to start. And who is the story about.

Cyrus and Darius have finally drifted off after thirty minutes of storytelling and singing. Energized by a day in the Wadi-Ram, riding across the desert in jeeps, exploring caves, running their thin fingers along the ancient glifs on stone the color of a dying rose, exhausted by the long drive, nervous from strange, dusty beds, and yet another new world, nervous from the separation from mother and grandmother, they have gone off to sleep unwillingly—the way children will, as if fearing that submission to darkness, that complete relinquishing of control. Susan is separated from us by a dingy hallway and two double-bolted doors. We are in a hotel in Aqaba and the night is desert cold. Outside the streets are still busy, still hum with commerce; and the scent of garlic and grilled meat mixes with the exhaust fumes that permeate the building. So we are apart again. As so many nights before. And our coming together is less frequent. Intimacy has given way to the bitterness of a long and desperate drifting apart—like two rafts connected by a slender cord, pulling apart, only to be jerked angrily back. In the room across the hall she sleeps next to her mother and she dreams. The next morning, heading to the bazaar to look for children's clothes, she tells me that her eyes hurt. That she was running toward a light all night and that she can't shake that blinding glare. She tells me less and less about her dreams. She has been hearing voices for months now. She tells me her poems are written by others. That she is a medium. And she tells me at first with wide-open eyes—eyes that stun every man and most women with their beauty and their dark, warm passion. But I know she is floating up and away from me like a piece of paper torn from a book by the wind, and I watch her the way people might watch a miracle—with reverence but also genuine fear—and not a little sense of one's own unworthiness; and so the stares always get harder, sadder. Her telling has lost hope. She doesn't believe she can reach me. And I guess she can't. It is always Ariel and Caliban. She, too much in love with the next world, and I, too much in love with this one.

Susan has come to Aqaba as she has come everywhere. Wanting to be open to the people and the world but also finding that it never lives up to her expectations. She is always disappointed in the frailty of others, though she doesn't give up on them easily.

The previous night we had gone down to the coast
and watched as the Muslim women swam fully
clothed, backlit in the evening light. Under the tent,
sipping tea, I found them tragically beautiful. But I
am a westerner and what seems confining and sad
to me is simply their world. A world they seem to
swim through with the comfort of knowing its borders. A world they step into as I step into the lake by
our house in Georgia—easily and without the shock
of cold. A different element but not a different temperature. My life with Susan has been a gradual
coming to terms with limitation—what I can and
cannot comprehend. Just how far I can go. And I've
learned it is not so far as either of us need. When
we make love, she looks away—far off, as if she is
looking into a future peace or reckoning. Alain, the
head of the Fulbright program, calls me "the satel-
lite," always circling Susan and her mother, boys in
hand. Never at the center. Taking what comes to me
without joy or anger or even humor. Just circling.
And I accept it. What else can I do? But Susan cannot. I can gauge her discomfort. Her desire to dive
in with these women. To be with them and understand them. But she will not go in fully clothed. She
never could. The point is total immersion. And so

she won't go in at all. She will sit and sip her tea pensively. Eyes stealing quick glances full of longing, then dropping down to the table, narrowing in fury at her saucer of tea—overfull and spilling with every accidental bump and jostle made by the evening revelers.

A mile down the beach, the resort hotel gleams in coral splendor. There, separated by a long concrete pier, the westerners swim silently in their bikinis, ignorant to what goes on here—the loud laughter. Louder arguments. The tables too close together. The pungent odor of cheap cigarettes and boiling leaves. As always she struggles. Who is she? Where does she belong? Married to a man who can't really understand her. Mother to children oblivious to anything but the moment. Daughter to immigrants who can't shake a longing for the gardens of their mothers and grandmothers, the huge dinner feasts, the music of Farsi. Wanting to dive in without giving in. To lose herself and keep herself.

Cyrus stands on the beach. He was cold. So in this photograph he wears my mother-in-law's long gold coat that reaches to the sand beneath him. And he looks exactly like some gaudy Christmas ornament. His head is bent down and he's smiling his closed-mouth, embarrassed sweet smile. Once a colleague, himself traveling headlong toward death, said to him "you are too beautiful for this world. Too beautiful for this world." But this day at the resort has been made for Cyrus, warm and happy with sandcastles, bright blue water and rides on the glass-bottomed boat in which he and his brother can marvel at the coral and bright fishes that swim through caves, their shadows and light. Even with his lids happily shut, you can tell he has his mother's eyes. Even cut short, his mother's hair. Like one soul in two bodies.

Cyrus stands at the top of the driveway in Michigan in his red snowsuit. Two years later, that suit will sit lonely in the basement of a rented house. Waiting for his father to claim it. But now, he puffs out warm breath and screams delightedly. As his father turns the corner, almost tipping the sled. Yanks hard on the rope and runs down the hill— boots slipping and stomping. His mother watches from the window and laughs brightly.

Susie and I are in a darkened room of the hospital. I hold a bedpan as she throws up into it, her skin as pale as a silent movie star's. Cyrus has just been born and he has been born hard into the world.

The nurse scribbles notes in a log book at the other corner of the room. Neither Susie nor I have seen the baby since they took him from her arms on the operating table. He had come through the wide cut in her abdomen, blue and not breathing. When I asked the doctor if he was OK, the nurse said quietly, *We just have to get him going.* Seconds passed. Susie was crying and her heart rate and blood pressure were dropping, her body reacting to the epidural. I thought I was about to lose them both right then.

Darius has a large stick and is drawing something in the sand. Every once in a while, he picks up a handful and throws it at his brother, who responds by clenching his teeth and shaking his fists inches beneath his brother's chin. Watching from the water's edge, I nervously hold back, rocking heel to toe in anticipation of a sudden attack. Cyrus has belted his brother before. Though I suspect his fury comes from an excess of passion—some kind of overflow of love and frustration. And I understand this. Understand it more than I want to admit to myself. A few months earlier in Georgia, Darius had accidentally locked himself in their room and Cyrus dropped to his knees in the hallway and started wailing. I'd never heard him cry so hard; deep desperate sobs. Though freeing Darius was easy enough—inserting one end of a paperclip into a hole in the door—Cyrus was upset for a long while afterwards, saying, "I couldn't live without my brother. I couldn't live without my brother," wrapping his thin arms around his sibling tightly enough to make him squeal in pain.

Like me, Akmed appears in only a handful of the hundreds of photos later saved from the chip in Susan's digital camera—staring out happily and squint-eyed from the bench on the glass-bottomed boat or holding the rope to a camel bearing my two sons—one laughing with delight, one screaming in fear. And yet, to me he was as much a part of the picture as anyone in the family. I'd never met anyone who I had so instinctively trusted and liked. One of the first truly genuinely spiritual people I had ever known other than Susan, our Palestinian teacher and guide had become a constant companion to us over the previous weeks. Ever since we'd met him on the bus to Jarash and hired him as a teacher of Arabic, we had felt more at ease with our lives in Amman. Akmed greased the wheel for us, warding off beggars and hostile young men. Returning from

a trip to the dead sea we had gotten stranded for
several hours in a small, Bedouin town poor enough
to be dangerous. To every angry beggar, every polit-
ical-minded station attendant, Akmed attested to
our good Muslim principles—even though it was
obvious to everyone that this blond-haired, blue-
eyed foreigner was about as Muslim as baseball and
hot dogs. But he deflected their anger, disbelief, and
frustration with a smile and grace that left everyone smiling, even those of us ignorant of what he
was saying. In fact, without Akmed, the trip itself
would never have been possible. We had suggested
the two-day adventure to him over Turkish coffee,
baklava, and Iranian gaz during a break in our language lessons, offering to pay for his hotel room and
food. Akmed, as always, was delighted to help. But
on the morning of our departure, he discovered that
there were no tour buses to Aqaba on Fridays—a
holy day to Muslims. I remember the knock on the
door, his bright, smiling eyes and busy hands, ges-
turing us out toward the beat-up minivan on the
sidewalk. At first I was hesitant. As with our trip
to Jarash, I worried about trying to see the country
as Susie had wanted—traveling as Jordanians did.
All the Fulbright information pamphlets had told

us to stick with tour companies and to stay in western resorts. We were also supposed to inform the Fulbright office of our movements at all times. But again, we would go off without anyone knowing where we were or how we would go there.

Susan's impulsiveness, a trait I had come to love in her, seemed a bit reckless now. Before the trip, both Susan and I had deflected the concerns of friends with similar statements. *To fear death is to fear life*, I told my department chair. And I believed it. I still do. But Susan's recent submersion into mysticism had left me worried. There was a fatalism that frightened me. In one conversation she told me that if something happened to us, she hoped we at least all died together. I stared at my two boys, just awakening to the wonders and terrors of this world and thought, *No*. Looking back on it, I realize that by that time, I had lost enthusiasm for following Susie on adventures that seemed always to be hers and not my own. That the idea of death did not disturb me as much as blindly following her towards it with our children, my children, towed behind us.

But Akmed settled me; he had brought a measure of peace into our married life. For years, Susan and I had cultivated an image of marital bliss.

In public I'd find her hand on my shoulder or my back, her fingers searching along my neck and up into my hair. She knew how to make me melt, how to turn my brooding intensity off for a time. And I would look over at her and remember the first time I had seen her walk into that Byron Seminar at Baylor University, dressed in a white-lace top and black velvet skirt. She dazzled me. Beautiful and brilliant and ten times the writer I would ever be. She was everything I ever wanted, and I wanted to be the perfect man for her. That I couldn't haunts me now. That my performance was good enough that she married me is almost harrowing. Recently my father-in-law told me that he was always against the marriage, that he knew that we were from different cultures and different classes of people, and that he knew that our marriage would only lead to tragedy for us both. And even up to a week before the accident, I had overheard my mother-in-law telling Susan that "the only reason you married Joel was because you slept with him." A statement that seemed loaded with bitter irony even then. Susan had always defended me in these kinds of arguments. But in all honesty, we both had strong misgivings that the marriage was a mistake. As early as a year into our life together, the cracks were showing in the foundations. No longer able to put a swaggering spin on my natural inwardness, my self-doubts, my frustrations with the academic profession, my inability to find fulfilling work, I became a dark and bitter man with whom to share a home. I believe that to keep from being pulled under with me, Susan pulled away. Our apartment turned silent. And Susie would sit for half a day in front of a blank canvas. For a time she began spending hours and hours with a local poet and artist, who, ironically, was more embittered than I was. But who doted on her. Who made her feel wanted and needed. I lost her heart and was never truly able to get it back again. Intimacy became a scheduled event. Something to be marked in Susan's daily planner to prove to both of us that our marriage was "fine." Heightening the tension was Susan's desperate desire to leave the United States. She had grown up in Switzerland and she wanted to return. Already depressed and poor with languages, I feared for my sanity should I follow her across the Atlantic. She didn't want to visit; she wanted to return to stay. And no matter how I tried I couldn't pursue that path. Even when I told her I would go with her, she knew that I didn't want to. That it would be something I was doing for her and that it would only make me more bitter. That was something she didn't want. So we rotted from the inside out.

But the outside looked wonderful. We made a beautiful couple walking into a function or a book-fair. And when we did readings together our mutual and genuine admiration for each other as writers and artists was received with warmth. Today, even talking with shared friends of our problems is difficult because we both played the roles of doting husband and wife so well. I often look back and wonder why the image of a perfect marriage was so important to Susan. In truth I think it was important to both of us. What we projected to others was the marriage we both wanted to have but couldn't have with each other—the marriage I hope to have one day. And there were so many things we genuinely loved about each other. To say that Susan was a great writer and teacher would be an injustice. She was one of a kind—like everyone else attending her readings or listening to her speak, I'd find myself slipping back easily into the admiration I had for her—the sense of worship and thankfulness you get when you encounter a truly open spirit, someone who can teach you of the world, push you into new territories. I'd like to think that we both made each other better writers, that we pushed each other and supported each other in our art. But admiration, even affection, is not love. Left to ourselves, in private, we fought a silent war of attrition, as if trying to force the other one to break the beautiful illusion we had created, to walk out the door and shatter the glass behind us. So many arguments ended with "why don't you just leave?" "What can I do? I'll do anything," and "it's too late; it's just too late." And it was. I remember at one conference, we were walking arm in arm, and a young writer came up to us with a sly smile, offering us a condom with her journal's name on it.

"Here," she said, "it looks as if the two of you might need one of these." We laughed, looked at each other, took the condom, returned her wink, and walked on. But we both knew the condom would stay in the bag of conference souvenirs. And when I returned to Georgia to vacate our home, there it was in the white plastic bag, staring up among pamphlets, stickers, key-chains. A black square with a circle inside of it—as cold as death.

I think we both knew that Jordan was a kind of last chance for us. A chance for Susan to reconnect with her heritage, a chance for me to prove that I could take that journey with her. Instead the fights grew more intense and with no neighbors to overhear us, no friends to impress, they became less private, sprawling out of the bedroom and into the hallways in front of my mother-in-law and the children. After one argument, Cyrus asked me, "Daddy, will you be sleeping somewhere else from now on?"

But with Akmed there, Susan and I seemed to slip back into that easy friendship we had before we got married. And even if it was role-playing, at least it was peace. So we stepped in behind Akmed as if he were the pied-piper himself. And if the van had no seat belts—well, neither did the cabs or any of the private cars. We were in Jordan. We were on an adventure. Akmed's friend turned to us with huge smile and waved us in.

There are no pictures of Susan in her bathing suit that day, but I remember. Anyone would. Susan was the type of woman that commanded attention. A year after we first met, Susan and I attended a reading at Baylor University for W.S. Merwin. She was wearing red velvet and when she entered the room, everyone in the auditorium, including the world-renowned poet, turned and looked. I would bet my life that he still remembers it. Though beautiful, Susan was always deeply embarrassed of her physical appearance. If people were staring at her, she'd ask me, "am I ugly today?" I'd tell her that people stared because she was beautiful, but I knew she never truly believed this, that there was nothing I could say or do to make her feel attractive and loved. I wasn't the one to do it. She thought her breasts were too small, her hips too wide, her nose too hooked. It is ironic that someone who so often lectured on the evils of western concepts of beauty was herself almost paralyzed by them. I remember her though, wading into the water, regal in a royal blue suit and wrap. She was gorgeous and tragic. Tragic because she knew that even being at that resort was a compromise—that by going there she had admitted to the unbridgeable distance between herself and the women on that beach the night before. Even on a journey of self-discovery, she was discovering herself as displaced, an outsider.

I stood in the Red Sea up to my knees, Cyrus shivering in my arms as Susan entered the water, her reflection elongating toward me. I remember eye contact. But even now, I can't imagine what she was thinking. I wonder if in the end she loved me. If I loved her.

On the drive home, Susan was still taking pictures. Out of the van window at the desolate and beautiful desert landscape as the sun descended. We were taking the long route home so we could see the Dead Sea again. I remember her being backlit—a living shadow—and I made some sort of sarcastic remark. Our banter was always fun. She turned to me and said something I can't remember. And I'd like to think she smiled.

I remember staring up at the stars. I was in unbelievable pain—as if someone had torn me in half. I remember a sudden burst of sound, people talking far away, what sounded like water rushing across stone—louder and louder. A river in New Hampshire coming through mountains. I remember thinking, *this is what it is to die.*

I was wrong.

CORPSE DESCRIPTION #1
The corpse is for a male child 7yrs of age. The corpse was totally rigid. The mortal spots were pale blue

and unclear. The corpse was naked and wrapped in a medical blanket. Total destruction of the skull and face bone. The brain was expelled from the cranium. Total destruction of brain. Contusions and abrasion of the right frontal chest, the scapula bone and right shoulder.

CORPSE DESCRIPTION #2
The corpse is for a female of 34 years of age. The corpse was totally rigid. The mortal spots located on the back were pale blue. The corpse was totally naked and wrapped in a medical blanket of white colour. The head was tied with bandage including the face. The lower extremities were also tied with bandages and cast. After removing the head bandage a big wound was seen located on the right cheek and extended upwards to the front and downwards to the left eye and nose bone. This contused wound is deep, coagulated blood blocked both nostrils. On the left side of the neck an oblique wound was noted.

I am fighting to wake up. It is just like those frightening dreams you have when you believe that you are awake or conscious but can't get yourself to open your eyes or move. I can hear voices; Arabic, French, then, "he's waking up." I shake myself hard and see Alain, the Fulbright coordinator. Alain looks serious, sad. He's holding my hand. *Joel, there's been an accident . . .*

I will tell you because you have to know, Joel. You have to know to understand what I have been through. You were asleep or unconscious or whatever. But I saw. And I still see. Always I see. I don't know how I live or why I live. But I saw. My mother-in-law is sitting in my parents' house in Sharon, Massachusetts on the gold couch, in the living room. Behind her, jays zip past the large picture window. I am finally home from the hospital. I have taken my first steps on crutches and am having a hard time concentrating. Initial reports by the associated press that I had a broken collar bone were inaccurate. I had shattered my hip, broken a joint that is supposedly the hardest in the body, and crushed the sciatic nerve. The surgery was eight hours long and complex and the recovery has been painful. The oxycodone and tramadol have entered my blood and I feel as if I'm floating, there and not there. My mother leans forward, with a dazed and frightened expression on her face—exactly as if she is about to watch an accident and can't do anything to stop it. And she is. And she can't. My father stands up and walks out of the room, fists clenched. *I will tell you because you need to undrastand me when I say to you about Darius, about Susie and her blood-money and what to do.* I am still the person I was before the accident. Still a little boy accepting and taking what comes to me. Why do I listen? Why don't I stop her? I know she is angry, lashing out at some undefined wall. I know this will hurt worse than my hip, worse than constant burning in my leg. Why did he survive she thinks? why does he live and not my daughter? In the hallway outside of our apartment in Amman, my mother-in-law said to my parents: *You need to remember that my daughter is dead. You still have your son.*

My in-laws had wrapped their lives around Susan. They would say of her often that they raised her *like a rose in a vase*. And their care for her spilled into my marriage. Whenever Susan needed her mother or father, they were there for her and they would stay in my home for weeks at a time at Susan's invitation, my father-in-law helping work out finances, my mother-in-law taking care of the children, doing laundry, cooking. What I could never express to any of them was the intrusion I felt in my life. The way this giving up of the rudder in my home left me feeling out of control, useless.

How I felt that their presence made it impossible for Susan and I to truly talk or work out our problems. *What I don't understand is, why, why did we get in that van. Why let Cyrus ride up front? It was like we got in the van and we were just SHUT. We couldn't talk, couldn't move. You never let the car move out of the driveway unless we were all buckled in. So why?* The first time my mother-in-law asked if she could take my son to Iran with her for two months, only a few days had passed since the accident. She and my father-in-law had made many requests very quickly, and I couldn't look in their eyes and say no. Susie and Cyrus were shipped off to Switzerland for burial before I really knew what was happening. I don't and didn't know if that was what she wanted. I knew that if I were ever to visit them, I'd have to fly across an ocean. And then my father-in-law—*I have a surprise for you, if you ever want to visit them, I'll pay for the flight.* No, I thought. No. I still felt it was my fault that they had died. That somehow my falling out of love with Susan, that her falling out of love with me, had set this in motion. Lying in bed, feeling immense guilt, compassion, physical pain, under the influence of high doses of morphine, I said, *Yes, whatever you want. Take him*. What I really wanted was someone else to take the burden I felt. I wanted my son kept safe *from me*. The way Susan and Cyrus were safe from me.

I was toxic, dangerous to everything and everyone I touched. *We were riding along in the van and for some reason Akmed—and what did we really know of him, why trust him, where did he come from—Akmed says, Let's take the long route back. And there he was with Cyrus leaning against his shoulder esleep. We all started dropping off. You were in and out.* I remember the darkness, the lights from the resort, reflecting in black water. *And then I could see it—small red lights, but we were going too fast. And I couldn't say anything. There was the truck across the road, and there was nowhere to go. The road dropped away on each side. So he just went straight in. And Susie sees Cyrus fly out.* She leans forward on the couch, arms spread. *And she says, Oh my God. And I don't understand this: the driver, he jerked the car and it spun so we hit the truck again and Susan, Susan was hit and you moaning, folding on top of her then underneath, beneath her, beneath the seats.* My mother later tells me that I am like stone. Like I'm not there, not hearing. She tells me how angry she was. But I need to hear. I need to get through this. To know. *And then I'm holding*

*Darius and running around the car to Susan and they
are yanking the two of you out. My God Joel, I've seen
things, I've seen things. They put you on the side of the
road. And they were asking me questions. Where was I
from. Who was I. Who to call.* The stars, the sound,
the rush. *And you made some sounds. I couldn't even
go to Cyrus. And Darius, he didn't cry until I put him
in the ambulance. I don't know how he broke his leg.
And then the helicopter came and I got in and flew with
Susan to the hospital. Watching Susan go. I was there,
I saw the line on the monitor go flat. I've seen things.
I've seen things.* There is more but I am no longer listening. I get up on the crutches, head to my room,
and start weeping in heaving gasps. I feel as if I will
pass out.

At the heart of every true story is a secret, is
a mystery. I once told my students that if a writer
could ever really tell the truth about the soul, that
story would be legendary—would move us all and
bind us all. But that truth is always just beyond us,
just out of reach. And even listening to my mother-
in-law, even retelling some of this to students in a
classroom in rural New England, I knew that this
story could not be true unless I could be true to it.
A few weeks ago I was going through Susan's poems

in an effort to pull together a posthumous manuscript. I found a poem called "Lovers"—a love poem
written to the poet from Nebraska. It was sad and
beautiful, the voice of someone in love with one person and married to another, the voice of a woman
desperate to leave a man who didn't understand
her, for a man who treated her like, well, a rose in
a vase. The poem was in a collection of unfinished
pieces she was working on in Jordan and the return
address in the upper left hand corner was for our
house in Georgia. Though I knew Susan's heart had
not been mine for many years, I did not know the
depth or term of her longing. Reading it, I felt no
anger. I would have been a hypocrite. The thought
of keeping it out of the manuscript didn't even occur
to me. It was too beautiful a poem. Too true and vital
to who she was. And I understood exactly what she
was feeling. I felt terrible sadness and sympathy. For
all the nights I had climbed to the roof in Amman
to sneak a cigarette and speak another woman's
name, then hop up on the low wall and walk it like
a balance beam as my older sisters had taught me
when I was barely three. For the moments I wanted
that desert wind to blow me off. For all the days in
Georgia I had thought of ways to step out of this

life, onto train tracks, into water, onto busy roads, to release the people I loved from the stain I put on them. What I felt went beyond understanding.

And if I can't tell you more, it is only because I am still in love and still in pain. And still trying to figure it all out. Still searching for some kind of answer. And to say more would be only to put names to things that have yet to come clear. To label and define what I cannot quite touch. Even now as I write this I know that I am not telling the story the reader wants to hear. What is wanted is a eulogy, an elegy, a lovely story about Susan, not of a broken marriage. I know that these truths are hard for everyone. And I apologize for its indecency—the inclusion of the corpse descriptions, the voyeuristic passages into intimate moments, the breaking down of the beautiful illusion so many seemed to enjoy. And I know that I am opening myself up to anger, to scorn. That I should play the broken widower for everyone's benefit, including my own. People will feel that they have to take sides, take their anger at Susan's loss out at someone, and I am readily available. But I can't play roles anymore. I can't afford to. These stories we tell matter. They have to matter. Otherwise we are all condemned to being merely satellites, always circling our lives and never quite making contact with the soul.

Just before my in-laws were set to leave Jordan with Darius, I changed my mind. There was no way I was going to let my son, having lost a mother, lose a father. He would stay with me. We would stay together. Because I couldn't face them and break my word, I asked friends from the American Embassy to break the news to them. It was the most cowardly thing I've done. And it was destructive. The embassy personnel feared that my in-laws would take Darius and not return. I didn't then and still don't believe that they would do such a thing. But I had moved so quickly from wanting to be rid of my son to wanting him with me forever that I was frightened. Afraid of their grief. Afraid that their sense of my guilt would drive them to do something wild, irrational. My mother-in-law came to visit me after she received the news and stood over my bed crying. *I want you to know how selfish I think you are,* she said. *I want you to know.*

Do I know anything? I believe that I am a better, stronger man than I was before this accident. I believe that some people almost need an event like this in their lives to find themselves. The fact of the deaths of Susan and Cyrus is brutal. I had thought they would both outlive me and I wish they had. Cyrus to awaken fully to the world. He deserved so much better. And Susan, so that she might have continued to be the writer, teacher and warm compassionate citizen of the world I once loved—that we all loved. And I know now that no one really knows what happens to you when caught in the midst of something like this. And that it is not all terrible. That there is still so much beauty in the world. Being in love again, having control of my life again, feeling like a good father and good man—these feelings send me into phases of euphoria and complete happiness. Then the fact of what happened comes crashing in, and sometimes the physical pain. And the manic swells and troughs take over. But they come less frequently every day. My son and I are good together. We love and need each other. We are happy.

The other day I dreamt of Susan. I was sitting on my sister's deck porch in Maine and she walked up to me, dressed in the white and black outfit she often wore around the house when relaxing or writing or painting. Her hair was braided. I looked at her and said, *Oh Susan, I'm so sorry.* She stared back.

I don't believe you. Then holding my hands, she looked straight into my eyes. *You do what you need to do to live your life.*

And I will.

SCREAM

FEBRUARY, 2005

SOMETHING IS WRONG. I am lying on the ice. It is mid-February, a year and one month since the accident. I have not yet screamed. That will come. It will come when it comes, when I have lost control of everything—completely at the mercy of my body. It will come as a shock as they roll me onto the aluminum x-ray table. An almost disembodied wail that seems as disconnected from me as any long low cry heard at the lakeside as boy. But I have not screamed yet. And though there is pain I am convinced I can rise up out of it, put my hands on the dock and pull up like a strong swimmer in a body-spray commercial—all teeth, muscles and wet shaking locks. I almost laugh. It's silly really. My son was having a playdate; he's still there. In the apartment. Watching *Ed, Edd, and Eddy* with his little friend Mikey. I had left the apple juice in the car (I always leave something behind), and so, bounced out the door, a little blinded by the early-evening winter sun—proud of how far I've come, cane-less, jacketless into the chill air. Earlier in the afternoon there had been a thaw and we had flown kites on the local football field at the bottom of the hill. But the temperature dropped in a matter of hours as I made popcorn, washed dishes.

So I hurried. Didn't notice the ice until I was almost horizontal with it. Then I hit. Felt something inside of me give.

"Unnnh," I said, just "Unnh," more surprise and outrage than pain. "Unnh."

"Daddy! Daddy?!" Darius is at the door.

"Its OK honey, Daddy's coming." I can't stand, so I crawl toward him, one leg trailing behind.

When the neighbor finds me, I have pulled myself up onto one leg by crawling up the side of the car. I had meant to hop into the apartment, but I am surrounded by ice. Trapped.

"I think I hurt myself a little," I say, calmly.

I don't scream, or even raise my voice. Perhaps I am still in shock, perhaps the drugs are working. Even when I lie on the gurney in the x-ray room, I stay weirdly quiet. When I do weep it is not because of the pain but because of frustration—the knowledge that all the hard work I have done, learning how to walk again, training the muscles to respond again, has come to nothing. I am useless to myself, my son—a cripple trapped inside the body's cage. I don't curse God, or like Job, regret my birth. After all, Job had a case. Job was a good man.

My case? It's only been a year and I have already begun a new relationship, am doing well in a new job, have learned to cook and play guitar. I've grown proud, independent. And I feel as if I am living not just a new life, but a false one. Though I still suffer nerve pain and bone pain—at times strong enough to keep me awake at night and grind my teeth until my jaw hurts—I feel each moment of life is an insult to their memories. I feel the strangeness of it all. The dark magic. I was a Fulbright scholar asleep in a touring van with my wife and sons on a late-night drive from Aqaba to Amman, sea water still in my hair, sand from the Wadi in my shoes. Someone parked a truck across the highway. And now I am a widower with a girlfriend. Where did they go, that family? What happened to that man? Why am I not haunted by his ghost? My happiness insults him too. So when it comes time to lift my body onto the raised, glistening, platform like a sacrificial animal in some ancient religion, I am nearly grateful.

Pain has a way of eliminating the past.

The orderlies, nurses, and medical technicians crowd around me, each taking a corner of the sheet on the gurney, the idea being to lift without touching—to distribute the pressure across my body. Staring up at the ceiling I remember a game I played as a boy. A child would lie in the center of a blanket and the other boys and girls would each grab a piece of the edge and lift it into the air. Then, gathering in close, they'd lower him nearly to the ground, until all at once the little hands would pull, the blanket would snap, and the body would fly up into the air.

"Ok, Everybody ready? Now. On a count of three."

I remember flying up and up again.

"One."

I think of Cyrus leaving the seat of the van, his shoulder and head hitting the glass first and splintering around him in a lethal rain.

"Two."

Did he feel pain? Did he have any idea what was happening to him as he flew up and up?

And did he scream?

THE NEVERLAND
JUNE, 2005

In the old days at home the Neverland had always
begun to look a little dark and threatening by bedtime.
Then unexplored patches arose in it and spread; black
shadows moved about in them; the roar of the beasts of
prey was quite different now, and above all, you lost
the certainty that you would win. You were quite glad
that the night-lights were on. You even liked Nana to
say that this was just the mantelpiece over here,
and that the Neverland was all make-believe.[2]

J.M. BARRIE

I IMAGINE THAT AT THIS MOMENT, staring at the
screen, at the message that came from out of nowhere and has now passed into some cold, tighten-
ing spot in my throat, I must look as a child does the
first time he is struck—that wide-eyed shock that
stops the breath and leaves the mouth open.

---

2. J.M. Barrie, *Peter Pan*. (New York: Penguin, 1987) 45.

It is snowing outside. My son lies on his back on the floor, laughing and heaving with breathlessness, his snowpants stuck around his ankles, his jeans darkening in the evening sky, blue patches where the snow has seeped in and melted into boiling, growing limbs. On the stereo Darius' favorite CD is playing an audio version of J.M. Barrie's *Peter Pan* and we are adrift in the gorgeous, languid phrasing. It has been a good day on the mountain—when the snow is heavy and wet and slick enough for sledding and snowmen and brightly thrown balls—when the delighted shouts of students emerge and disappear in and out of drifts and milky distances. And though I've been conscious of what is missing from the picture, I am also aware that there will be time for the demons and the darkness that will come when it comes on its own accord like an impudent friend stepping through a doorway during a domestic argument or just before lovers begin to love. It will come. It will come when I'm making a cup of coffee early in the morning, the scent pulling backward to a moment in our first apartment, in the kitchenette, and I can see the snow falling into the courtyard behind our back porch and hear the squeak of the baby rocker rocking Cyrus to sleep; it will come when I'm in the car, on the way to Wal-Mart to pick up apple juice, or a new toothbrush, buzzing in over the radio in the form of a Beatles song—Susie's favorite group; it will come when I am giving Darius a bath and suddenly I'm in Jordan again after three days without hot water, finally able to get the kids warm and clean, reveling in their nakedness and in being together shrieking and splashing, laughing and crying. Brothers. And I know it will come when it always does, long after I've sung my son, my life, to sleep. When the bills have been paid and grades given and I am left to luxuriate—to sit back in my grief like a child in the backseat of a car who can drive to the same place again and again but never learn how to get there—simply sink into the soft cushions, listen to a music chosen by other hands and watch the world pick up speed and blur to the left and the right and rush behind me as if pulled into a hole in the sky.

One thing it doesn't need is a helping hand. A shove. Or even the most gentle reminder.

"Just a Question" the message header reads, and when I see that it is from an old friend, I feel trepidant. I've become a hard man to surprise since the accident. I've grown suspicious as Job of comfort and comforters. In the hospital room, for months after the crash, I had learned to accept graciously the visits and visitors filing in—ministers, old friends, family I had not seen for years, even those who had merely heard of what had happened in the hallway and wanted to touch the edge of my blankets as if the robe of some bishop, some dying saint. And it was easy then to play the role. I could do little else—in teeth-grinding pain from a shattered pelvis and a crushed nerve that shot a continuous fire through my legs which only the strongest painkillers—the kind that make you sweat and that pull the moisture from your mouth—could come near—I sat quietly, spoke quietly, let them bask in whatever it was that pulled them to me. At the time I accepted it like spring rain—a natural phenomena that was a sign of the basic goodness of people and of the earth. And I would tell the minister, my father, my sisters, anyone who would listen that I was not angry, that in fact, if anything, the genuine compassion that surrounded me reminded me of how blessed I still was.

And yet, after a while, each sad, expectant face became like a pressure on a sore. Their stares frightened me. Their pity frightened me. What do they want from me, I thought? I was not Job—the pious

favorite of God, wrongfully and senselessly pun-
ished. And I was no saint. I used to tell my students
that the expectations of a community were always
around us. That even the teacher walking into the
classroom feels this. And so do the students. There
are always rules, spoken and unspoken for how we
are meant to behave, talk, move, dress. And as much
as we complain of these rules and try to shake them
from us like heavy snow, we long for them. They
keep us from falling into panic—into the despair
that one encounters when faced with what Sartre
named radical freedom—that moment when we
realize that we can travel any road we want, but
have no guidance, no map, no way of knowing
which way is best. And the rules, the codes are both
a comfort and a trap. If we can live up to expectations, we succeed. If not? *If even one of these people
really sees me*, we ask ourselves, *would they still feel
pity, or throw stones?* So each of us struggles not only
with a desire for freedom in the face of a need, for
belonging, but with the accusations coming from
within. We walk amid our communities feeling
fraudulent—as if everything we are is constructed,
is false, is a hoax. *What would they make of my anger,
my confusion, of the guilt I've carried with me like a*

huge sack of sand strung from my neck, I often wondered. Not only the guilt of having let my son sit in
the front seat of a van without a seat belt. That was
forgivable—mere neglect. But for all the other sins.
The bitterness that lived in our house, in his house,
for half his life. For the suppressed frustrations that
sometimes overwhelmed me and burst upon him
like sudden hail. For the man I had become before
the accident. As much as I loved my son, as much
as he loved me, I know that I was also a kind of
darkness to him. Where his mother was a source
of joy and warmth, I was the source of discipline.
Where Susan was always an affirmation, I was
the one who said *no*. *No* to the roughhousing with
his brother, *no* to staying up that extra hour, *no* to
sleeping between us in our bed (though ultimately
relenting when there was so much between Susan
and I that it hardly made a difference). The adult in
Neverland who was always asking the child to stop
dreaming and thus threatened to destroy the dream
of Neverland itself.

The truth was that I was always waiting for
someone, anyone, to come storming into the room,
finger pointed like a barrister at Nuremburg, shouting *J'Accuse*. But no one ever did. So I desperately

wanted these visitors and feared them—fearing the judgment I believed I deserved and simultaneously hoping it would arrive, simply to put me out of the misery of anticipation—needing the reassuring touch of hand in hand, and wanting somehow to take wing and fly away.

And I wonder if that is what I've been doing, just trying to run from those eyes ever since. All the while knowing that I really can't. Because to run from them would be to run from myself—from my guilt. And that trails you like a vapor.

So I have been waiting for this e-mail like a sniper behind a bush. And if I am shocked, it's the shock of finally having the target right in front of me. The letter begins kindly, offering praise for letting Darius spend two weeks with his grandparents, before quickly and sharply moving toward its point. Apparently my friend has heard from my in-laws that I am not going to go with them to visit Susan and Cyrus's gravesite on the anniversary of the accident. *I know that your life has changed and you have formed new alliances,* the letter reads. *But some things are incomprehensible to us. I hope you know, Joel, that many of us are still thinking of her and Cyrus almost every day (she clearly had more friends than even she knew!). We cannot do much for her other than preserving her beautiful legacy, praying for her family and her gentle soul, remembering her and her short, too short, life. But you can.*

What shocks me even more is my own fury. The rage I feel coming up. Of course I can't go to Switzerland for the anniversary of the accident. I work now, am the only means of support for my son, and the trip would take a week away from my job. We are only beginning to get our feet under us. And a twelve-hour plane flight across the Atlantic to visit a graveyard is hardly the best thing for a four-year-old. It would do nothing but cause emotional confusion and pain for both of us. To say that it would set us back is almost too obvious. But that is not the source. It doesn't quite justify what's going on inside of me. *HOW DARE YOU TELL ME HOW I SHOULD GRIEVE?* I write. *YOU DON'T KNOW WHAT I GO THROUGH EACH DAY. THIS WAS NOT THE ACT OF A FRIEND* and finally *DO NOT CONTACT ME AGAIN.*

With only a little hesitation I position the little arrow over "send" and press down, feeling both relief and nausea. That sense I always have when I send an e-mail I know I might regret—the locked

door slamming shut with the keys still in the igni-
tion. *What has happened to me*, I wonder? I feel
like a villain, waving his hook beneath the victim's
nose, and worse, I feel giddy about it. I feel good.
As if some quiet nagging voice within me has taken
shape, become a real wall to beat against, a prison-
guard to overwhelm.

Of course it has everything and nothing to do
with this particular message. My friend has not just
hit a nerve but stepped on a land mine.

It has been nearly a month, and I am still reel-
ing a bit from Darius's visit to New Jersey and my
in-laws. He's been struggling with nightmares since,
refuses to sleep with the light off, asks me every day
if I'm going to die. And I struggle with the guilt of
leaving him in their misery and with the guilt of not
leaving him with them enough, and with the guilt
of not being able to withstand their barely restrained
anger towards me—one couched within the protes-
tations that they love me like a son and in statements
like, *Even if you get married again tomorrow I will
still be your mother-in-law*. A statement of love? An
act of self-defense? My in-laws' little ranch-house
in Saddle River has become a real symbol of unre-
solved grief—a shrine to death with photographs of

the lost hung from every open corner and bare space on the wall, a place where a DVD of a little funeral in an empty church in Switzerland plays over and over again all night long on a bedroom television the size of a small package. The place I left my son for two weeks because I couldn't say no to their pain, because I wanted him to have two sets of grandparents and because I'm weak. Still weak. Or is it compassion? Cowardice? Our relationship has always been a hard one to unravel and since the loss of their only daughter it has only become more difficult. What happened to us, to them, is beyond anyone's ability to understand. Do I blame them? Am I bitter? Or is their grief a kind of challenge to me? A mirror that shows me how I too, ought to think and feel and can't or won't.

In the car, after picking my son up from his weeping Poppa and Bibi, I was given a very powerful lesson in how environment can affect a child. Even as they receded into the world of the past behind us, Darius began to voice new questions in a language that was new to him. From the backseat the words rolled one after another: *Daddy when are you going to die? Daddy can we take an airplane to heaven to see Mommy and Cyrus? Daddy I want to die.*

I want to die soon so I can be with my brother. Can you die with me? Daddy I know I'll never see my Mommy again. How long will it be until I die? I don't know that any parent is equipped to deal with hearing his four-year-old express a desire to die—especially when that parent has already lost a son. It was like having some vital part of me—the soul perhaps, or what passes for the soul—spooled out of me from the gut. But I knew what to do. How to turn the dark thoughts into a kind of magic, to spin grief and transform it like some magician turning a black handkerchief into a dove.

So I told him a story of how, when his mother was six months pregnant in the house in Michigan and literally bursting with him, she spent hours putting together a train for him and his brother, painting a sea and islands on an old door, gluing down the tracks. How I had kept it and when we got back we could take it out of storage and set it up again. I told him how magical it was to have them watching over him like two gentle angels, sending him happy dreams and butterfly kisses.

His eyes glittered darkly in the rearview mirror, his face rounding with a grin. I wondered what was really going on behind that happy smile. Would either one of us ever be whole again? Would real happiness be allowed for us?

The CD drones on in the background: *I don't know whether you have ever seen a map of a person's mind. Doctors sometimes draw maps of other parts of you, and your own map can become intensely interesting, but catch them trying to draw a map of a child's mind, which is not only confused, but keeps going round all the time.*[3]

As I watch Darius push his trains carefully along the wooden tracks set up on the floor of our two-bedroom apartment, I can't help but wonder what is going on in my son's mind. I don't know if Darius makes the connections between himself and the lost boys longing for a mother. It's always hard to tell. But it is not lost on me. And I am having a hard go at holding it together. The language pulls me in. Barrie is my kind of writer, lush and romantic, with just a touch of irony, of playfulness. But mostly he understands. For all his weaving of fantasy, he understands our most basic desires.

Of all delectable islands, the Neverland is the snuggest and most compact; not large and sprawly, you

---

3. Barrie, *Peter Pan*. 6.

know, with tedious distances between one adventure and another, but nicely crammed. When you play at it by day with the chairs and table-cloth, it is not in the least alarming, but in the two minutes before you go to sleep it becomes very nearly real. That is why there are night-lights.[4]

As I give in to the phrasing, I really do feel as if I'm pulled along into that world, that if I squint my eyes, I can almost see it, almost recreate it here in this snug, compact little apartment of light and warmth that I've created for us. I sometimes wonder if Cyrus is Peter to my son. A boy of unreal bravery, who even when faced with drowning has the thought that *dying will be a wonderful adventure.* A boy who will never grow up, who exists eternally flying outside of time and pain, fighting evil pirates on some imaginary island. Perhaps that is where Susie and Cyrus have gone for him. That island of comfort where boys play in their pajamas all day and good is good and evil is evil and the only adults are the villains. Except for Susan, reading to them as they sleep, mother to the lost boys. I smile at the thought. A beautiful way to explain heaven to a little boy.

---

4. Barrie, *Peter Pan*. 7.

Or even to myself. For the Neverland is not only the destination of children. It is the destination to which we all long to travel but is always just beyond us. And that is because the Neverland is really a fulfillment of a contradiction. A place that can only exist in the imagination where the desire for community and the urge for freedom is resolved by a trick of light. For children this is manifested in the desire to escape the world of multiplication tables, chores, and household rules and into the land of play, far removed from the watching eyes of parents and teachers. But for adults that desire to both free oneself from praise or judgment and yet still belong to something is equally profound. Especially among the suffering.

Weeks after getting out of the hospital, my foot still swollen from a blood clot, my mind still packed in the cotton gauze of tramadol and oxycodone, I would travel with my sister every week to Neverland's photo negative—the world Barrie only touches upon through implication—the small space in the backroom of an Episcopalian church in Marlboro where the parents of the lost boys and girls sit in a circle holding hands, needful not of sympathy or scorn, but mere understanding, not so much community as communion. The group was named Compassionate Friends and I sat with them as they wept over memories of the lost. Some had grown accustomed to the pain and wore it with relative ease, like a heavy overcoat; others were still struggling to stand or even sit without crushing beneath its weight. In the book-lined alcove, in chairs designed for children, the stories of grief were told. One couple had a son crushed beneath a car when the jack that held it collapsed. Another's daughter was thrown from a vehicle driven by her drunk ex-boyfriend. This woman lost an infant to cancer. This man's son leaped from a building at school. A few sentences each to tell the story of grief that cannot be told in a lifetime or even understood by the most patient and committed archeologist of the soul. If I were to say, *I was in an accident in Jordan. We were traveling in a van from Aqaba to Amman. A sand truck was parked across the road. I don't remember much. I was asleep in the back when it happened. Cyrus was thrown through the windshield. Susan, my wife was crushed in the impact. My pelvis was crushed . . .* would that explain things? Even in this circle of empathy, I could feel people filling in the gaps, imposing their own stories, assuming what I felt, what I must feel.

It must be like surviving a war, someone said. *You didn't just lose a child but your wife, too. It's like you have shell-shock.*

And so, even in a circle of compassionate friends I wanted to run, because I could never make what I actually felt line up with what I thought I was meant to. And after a time, I stopped going to the meetings. Because how could I explain what was happening in my heart to people who thought they already knew? Or who thought they knew what should be there?

Could I tell them what I felt was not shock but dull fury? That my first feeling after the accident was not so much sorrow but abandonment? As if Susan had somehow stolen Cyrus from me. Taken his hand, sprinkled the fairy dust and floated off, leaving me in the cold blast of air, coming through a window?

And for just a moment, I am back in the military hospital in Jordan. I have been in and out of consciousness and have really seen no one since Alain, my Fulbright coordinator, told me what happened in the ICU two days ago. Since then, it's morphine and sleep. No one has even bothered to clean me yet. Though there is no mirror here, I see my reflection in the bedpans and the polished aluminum support-

ing beam of the morphine drip. Across my forehead
is an ugly scar and blood is caked around a thick,
black, jagged row of stitches. *Not exactly a profes-
sional job,* I think. *But who gives a shit now anyway.*
In the last years of my marriage, Susan would often
point out my Cro-Magnon brow, blaming it for both
of her difficult pregnancies. I could never really
tell if the banter was playful or bitter. I look exactly
like Karloff's Frankenstein. There is a strange urge
to laugh.

My father-in-law is standing by the bedside,
weeping. I have not seen my mother-in-law yet.
My own family is flying to me, somewhere over the
Atlantic. I have no idea what to say. It was my fault,
you see; there's no getting around it. There were no
seat belts. Cyrus was in the *front seat.* I'm the father.
It's my fault. Dear God. It's my fault.

Grief is never about the event, but about everything that happened before the event. The anger,
the guilt, the outrage are located in what we would
forget if we could—those flashes of memory, good
and bad, that complicate our understanding of
what happened. And these are not available to the
community. What they see, what they experience
through a victim, is the story they desire—whatever

narrative they need so that they may deal with their own lives.

So I have learned that I represent something to people. A phenomenon that made me uneasy even in Jordan where I was visited, it seemed, by almost everyone. The king's brother, the American ambassador, every doctor in the hospital, each nurse. Every night, student Fulbrighters would come to talk with me, take care of me—even shaving me at one point. People I hardly knew would stop by to play music for me, or talk politics, or simply sit quietly and stare from a dimly lit easy chair in the corner. Staring back at them, I was grateful for the breaks in isolation. Surely the worst moments were when I was alone in that room, in pain, with the demons. But I couldn't help but wonder what I was to these people—most of them knowing nothing of me but my situation. They were certainly driven by compassion. I have no doubt. But I've also learned that victims of all stripes represent us all in some way. And I have learned that I am either monster or superman to the watchful eyes of the comforters. At the hospital, I was told how peaceful I seemed, how gracious I was, how kind and good. No one thought that just perhaps that saintly demeanor had more to do with massive doses of narcotics than with the hand of God. But where there is no meaning, people will seek one out.

In some ways that is the very nature of the artist—the shaper. The mundane reality of an accident and the damage it causes does nothing for us if we can't shape it, give it substance and purpose. In her non-fiction classes my wife used to tell her students: *Let us take this material ugly as it is, and make something beautiful of it.* So non-fiction derives much of its power from that tension between the transformative nature of art and the desire to hold onto the truth—to be as honest as humanly possible. And the truth always seems to exist on the very edges of language, of story. Not because we can't deal with too much reality but because that is how we do deal with it. We sit on the edge of the bed and say, *Tell me a story*, and we want it to be a story of *great distances and starlight*. We want magic. *Take this lump of clay and blow life into it,* we say to the great Magician. Make me more than a child. Give me fairy dust and a star by which to plot my course. And a star for my destination. Of course this is what I'm doing and trying not to do for Darius and for myself and for the reader of this essay. I am creating a meaningful story of my life and myself. None of it is true exactly, but is as truthful as possible; it is the act of truthmaking which is by nature inexact, complex and bursting at the seams of the symbols, images, characters and turns of phrase with which we seek to trap it. And so I shape the clay, tell and retell my story, shape and reshape myself, until sometimes I feel that I can't really be a man any longer—even to me. I feel as if I can't shake loose this role, this situation—like some method actor locked in a part.

You see, the victim suffers for all of us, and he heals for all of us. It is through his sins, his pain that we are somehow cleansed, and through his return to life that we experience resurrection. And the wages for his supplication to misery for an appropriate length of time before finding the other side of it in some—preferably celibate—rebirth, are sympathetic gestures—kind words—a neighbor dropping by bearing chocolate chip muffins. And the phone calls, and the e-mails.

The sufferer represents something—a stand-in for those who fear at their core that what could happen to him could happen to them too.

The sufferer symbolizes something—the constancy of love in the form a grieving widower who spends the rest of his life mourning his loss.

The sufferer does something—maintaining himself as a living reminder of all that was once so beautiful.

Mostly he suffers.

That is his purpose.

He cannot be full of faults and talents, purity and perversions, strength and weaknesses, because that would mean that the world has indeed moved on and he is merely, if tragically, human. The sun has gone down and come up again. And there's nothing we can do to stop it. Even the most brutal tragedy does nothing to interrupt the onward rush. And so a child's bright smile seems almost indecent in the face of the loss of his mother and his brother.

Darius is now tugging at my sleeve. He wants marshmallows in his cocoa. This is not the first time my son has had to deal with an interruption of his life with me. How many times now have I been cooking dinner, planning a trip to the children's museum, playing hungry hippos on the floor, only to have the phone ring and someone on the other line saying, *Oh Joel how are you; I've been thinking of you and Darius*—the voice on the edge of weeping or already breaking down as if someone were gasping for air. What they don't want to hear is the truth. They want to experience my grief, to weep with me over the phone. To trade stories of Susie and the kids and have a good long cry. They do not want to hear: *Darius is doing wonderfully. He loves his school and he has playmates all around him. I love my job and we are doing well. We are surrounded by love.* I know. I've tried to tell people this only to confront an awkward silence. This is not how it's meant to be, you see. But there is no way to be. Just expectation in the face of mystery.

A memory:

It was about four years ago and I was traveling by greyhound to prepare our new house in Georgia for Susie and the kids before we all took the station wagon down as a family. I was waiting in a Nashville bus stop at about 3 a.m. The cafeteria-like space was full and active—with the activity of sleepwalkers: exhausted travelers trying to unfold dollar bills and stuff them into vending machines, trying to catch a few winks against a wall, trying to position themselves in the right place, near the doors, so when the bus was fueled and clean and ready, they could find choice places in line and choicer places on the busses, near the doors, against the windows, far from the stink of the toilet in the back. I was simply trying to shake off the weight of my own concerns when everything seemed to come alive in a burst of activity and shouting: *Mister, are you alright? You need a doctor?—somebody call an ambulance.* There by the ticket counter, a man had dropped to his knees, a few dollars spread out on the floor by one of his hands, an old leather pouch a few feet away. My first thought was that he had had a heart-attack and people were responding with appropriate, even effective, concern. But soon it became clear that his health wasn't the problem. He lifted his chin and we could see that he was weeping. When people began to realize that he was not dying, but "merely" suffering, they backed off—leaving about three feet all around him. They looked away, spoke in low whispers to each other. No one touched him, or approached him any longer, as if they feared that by entering his pain, it might become their own. Or maybe they were scared—*is he insane? Is he dangerous or contagious?* By appearances you wouldn't have thought so. Though not wealthy, he was well dressed, clean-shaven, old, but not old to the point where you wondered if his mind had gone. Perhaps some were angry, felt duped, upset that their real concern for his health was misplaced. And of course, there was the simple indecency of it. A bus stop has its own rules. It is not a church or a graveyard. It is not a hospital waiting room. Perhaps the man had offended us merely by breaking the rules of grief. Eventually he got up and walked to the restroom, a bit wobbly but composed. I didn't see him again. But I think of him. How many of us hold in our pain as if embarrassed by it? How many seem even more embarrassed at the sorrow of others? We don't know what to do with our hands. We don't know what to say. Half wanting to know what he suffers, half wanting our happy ignorance, we end up calling him "crazy" or "tragic," fixing him in a formulated phrase, as Eliot once wrote, then moving on to our destinations.

These days I think less about the crowd than the man as he walked off. I wonder if even he wanted to run from himself and what he had become in that instant—the way I do sometimes now. My life is incomprehensible to me. Each day, every day is a reckoning with the reality and surreality of my condition. A coping with how much can change in an

instant, with the change that comes of one poor decision in a moment. And it seems impossible to grasp.
A friend will say to me suddenly, over dinner, *I can't
imagine what its like to be in your head.* And I say,
*don't try. What good could it possibly do you to imag-
ine it? Enjoy your children. Don't ever think of what
it would be like for them to die. You can't prepare for
it anyway.* And you can't. You try to reconcile your
life now with your life then, and you can't. You live
each moment as if you've been dropped into another
dimension. As if in the real world the driver of the
van saw the sand truck parked across the highway
early enough and swerved around it. And we were
shaken out of dreaming to shocked but relieved
faces, perhaps even a joke or two about how close
it was. And the memory became something to tell a
story of, over dinner, among friends.

Instead, I must begin with this. It was Friday
morning—our last weekend before we began teach-
ing at the University of Amman, and Akmed, our
new Palestinian friend and interpreter, came to the
door. He never knocked, but waited for us to somehow know he was there and we always did. Because
we were always waiting for him. Akmed, our interpreter, our guide. And this time we were waiting

with more anticipation than ever. We were excited because we'd never been to Aqaba—and it seemed a place of great mystery and ancient fables. Cyrus was leaping around the apartment, jumping off of couches, brandishing a plastic sword. And there was Akmed, holding out his arms, smiling broadly as my mother-in-law pulled the door inward, saying, *Good news; no dirty tour bus today. I've found a friend who has a van. Much better for the lady, much more comfortable.* I had no objections, no concerns. I'd learned with time to simply go with the flow. And Susan, with her long flowing hair and quick bright eyes, always had a current all her own—forceful and fast, sweeping everything along. So when we got into the car with too few seats and no belts, I said nothing. Did nothing.

I can remember the exact color of the marble stairs, the light brown jacket that Cyrus wore, the way he clutched his teddy bear, Winky, to his chest, then swung through the door and down the steps. His huge brown eyes. His delicate wrist. How a burst of blackbirds exploded from the tree above us, scaring Darius into tears.

Though if I were to be truly, brutally honest, the story, my story of grief, would begin elsewhere—

perhaps with the night in the freezing apartment when Cyrus refused to do his homework. He was screaming and flailing. Begging to watch his cartoons and play. He had regressed since entering Amman's Montessori school, suddenly unable to complete the most basic assignments that back in Georgia took ten minutes at the most. I was standing off to the side as I always did when my mother-in-law was there, unable to participate, for every attempt at discipline was met with scorn. There were times when I would beg Susan and her mother to leave the house so that the chaos would cease. And it would. With the closing of the door, the two boys would calm down and play with each other at make believe, almost never fighting. I'm not certain if this was because they feared me—I was the only one who would give a time-out or even speak sternly to them—or because they no longer had to fight for their mother's attention, negative or otherwise. But with the three of us in the house, and with none of us enforcing a consistent set or rules, we were always on the verge of wildness. My mother-in-law sat near him, arm around his shoulder, getting more and more frustrated. Susan sat across the table, finger planted firmly on the page. Then, out of nowhere, Cyrus's arm went up in anger, hitting my mother-in-law in the side of the face, knocking off her glasses. Then what? I don't remember, only Cyrus flying through the air and onto his bed and me standing above him, catching sight of myself in the mirror, blind with anger. I didn't hurt him. But I scared him. Cyrus's face was a mask of fear. And I am haunted by his face and my own. By his shock and my anger.

These are the sources of real grief and real pain. The regrets. The worst moments of our lives with those we've lost coming up to accuse us from within.

So as I sit and stare at the computer screen I am really staring at my own guilt, my own self-loathing, and I am trying to beat it back, but I lack the tools. How can we fight ourselves? We can't. The best we can do is attempt to move forward somehow. To adjust to who we are at this moment, and be as honest as we can about who and what we've been. Then try to do better.

At a dark time people came to me for comfort, both to bring it, and, I imagine, to find it. To know that there was something still left, still shuddering, the way sunlight appears to shiver on the sea after the sun is gone. But soon that too fades. All I wish to do is be allowed to follow that slow inevitable descent. And appear, perhaps, rising over other distant oceans.

If you shut your eyes and are a lucky one, you may see at times a shapeless pool of lovely pale colours suspended in the darkness; then if you squeeze your eyes tighter, the pool begins to take shape, and the colours become so vivid that with another squeeze they must go on fire.[5]

And what then? What will be there? I wonder. On the other side, will the pain be less sharp? Will I find a way to look at my wedding photos without weeping? Will I be able to go sledding with my son and not think continually of his brother? And even as I struggle with that string snapped in my chest, even as I hold down the pain in my shattered hip, even as I struggle blindly with the many roads and avenues and back alleys of my mind and memory, will I still bear quietly the intrusion of the friend walking by, saying, *Joel, you look like you don't have a care in the world?*

People see what they want to. I am for them what they need me to be. Broken or healed. Saint or demon. Hero, Villain, Job. Sometimes I envy

---

5. Barrie, *Peter Pan*. 86.

Cyrus and Susan, not because they are at peace but because they are beyond watchers and the watching. They can't be touched where they are. My oldest son will never grow up and Susan will never grow old. They will swim, beautiful and whole, with the mermaids in the bright lagoons of a child's memory.

But I have stopped searching for Neverlands, for magic. Reality is all around me and its strangeness, its over-ripeness is both terror and joy enough. It is not a matter of facing or not facing my grief but deciding what to do within it, how to respond. The grave markers in Switzerland will not make their loss more or less real, neither will my visiting bring to others continuance or closure.

When I sat and watched the video of the funeral with my in-laws one night in August, staring in painful disbelief at my son's little white coffin and the larger silver vessel in which Susan sailed, I found no solace, no peace, and no increase in pain—if increase in pain could be possible—just a sense of nausea, some bleak awareness that these images would be with me forever. Even the digger loading in the dirt (yes, they filmed even this) and the backhoe flattening the mounds above them could not bury that. And I wondered what possible good I had done myself in forcing my eyes upon the little screen.

I keep rereading the end of my friend's e-mail: *Wishing you peace of mind and good health. To little Darius a universe of prayers and all my love.*

Peace comes, acceptance comes, if it comes at all, with the gradual adjustments we make each day to a new condition, as if adapting to frigid water. And continuance is only our decision not to drown. It is change—is motion. A contradiction of itself. Contradiction itself. Because that is all that life allows us. All that can remain the same is what we frame and place on the mantle like a sepia toned photograph of Cyrus and Darius at play on the beach in Savannah, or the black and white 8x11 portrait of Susan I have placed by Darius's bed to watch over him as he sleeps.

In the end, Barrie's *Peter Pan,* like Homer's *The Odyssey*, like my story and Darius's, is a story about a journey and a return. Wendy and the boys must give up Paradise to enter the adult world—the fires of the imagination receding not only from sight but slowly from memory. Darius will remember little except for what we tell him, except for what he reads in his mother's poetry books when he is old enough to understand them, what he reads in the long spaces in the halting, painful memories of family members. I hope it will not be dust and dirt and the image of a backhoe on a television screen. But Darius is not cursed by memory; he is blessed by its loss.

At the end of his grand adventure, Barrie writes: *And thus it will go on, so long as children are gay and innocent and heartless.*[6] A cryptic passage, unless we understand that the cruelty of children is only perceived by the adults they leave behind. It is in its very lack of intent that we feel its sting. Adults look at the child who lost his mother, playing happily on the floor of a two-bedroom apartment in New Hampshire and they feel the outrage of neglect and abandonment. How could he be happy with his mother gone, his brother tragically lost? A child's cruelty is a kind of transcendent selfishness that we wrest from them at our own peril. It is what one finds when one has not so much let go of the past but does not acknowledge it all. In the blinding moment of sunlight glancing off snow on a winter's day, there *is* no past. And the child rises up and up as if he has forgotten we were ever there.

---

6. Barrie, *Peter Pan.* 192.

I am no child; my memory is singed by fires beyond the imagination. When I close my eyes I see the dark penetrating stare of my wife; I see my son. I imagine the bursting of glass and a young body flying off and into space. And I feel the terror of guilt. This is the brutal reality of adults whose minds eat them alive, dark thoughts blossoming like cancer cells. I know that I cannot have my son's peace and that too much of my joy is lived through him. Even Odysseus wept.

But each day, every day I become stronger. And part of that strength is not only in taking up the burden but in having the strength to set it down. To say no to those who would have me carry it for them. My responsibilities are elsewhere. Darius opens the door and steps out into the snow sled in hands, saying, *Daddy, let's go* and laughs. And I will follow that laughter as far as it will take me—even if it leads me off the end of this earth. Who knows what bright lagoons shimmer in the distance.

RUINS

SEPTEMBER, 2005

FRIDAY IN AMMAN is the Sabbath day, so very little is open or active—other than the prayers coming over the loudspeakers, and the numerous mosques, whose spires reach up all around us. Five times a day, every day, the call to prayer floats over the rooftops from dozens of loudspeakers, each slightly ahead or behind the other and echoing off the sides of buildings and through the valleys, so it sounds like a crowd of angels calling you home toward some kind of reckoning.

On these days I take the boys for walks through some back lots and up the hillside roads behind our apartment. We live in Jebel-Amman, literally Mountain-Amman, on the side of one of the many steep hills that form the city's landscape. And even after a month of living in this churning city, I can't shake the feeling that I could uproot, tumble down into the valley and be lost in the vacant lots and low-lying troughs in the land dotted and shining with rubble.

* * *

I can still feel the pressure of the umbrella stroller in my palms, though it's hard to believe, staring at him from the light of the hallway, that this boy, curled into sleep on his mother's old bed, was once that child. His hair, once long and curled as any young girl's, is now cropped tight and matted against his forehead with August sweat. Susie would hate it. She loved his hair. Cyrus was nearly four before he had his first "big boy cut." And though Darius is only a year older than his brother was on the day of the accident, he seems almost larger than Cyrus now. And what have I become?

Now?

Then?

Here. In his grandparents' house, surrounded on all sides by the howling August storm, those distinctions slither in and out of time and place like something venomous in the underbrush.

"Hate and love," my mother-in-law said, staring at me in the living room, waiting for some reaction. And for once she did get one, her words cracking the reinforced concrete calm that I adopt when the subject of Susan's journals arises.

"Hate and love. Love and hate. I've never heard anything like it."

The word "hate" is not one I allow myself. Especially when referring to Susan. She is gone, and to hate the dead, to love the dead—it all seems somehow obscene. She is a part of me, like Cyrus; that is all. I don't try to untangle any further. What I felt for Susan was what I understood love to be.

"How could she be so unhappy and us not know? And suicidal. She mentions suicide three times."

I catch my breath as if to speak. To say, *she wasn't the only one*. To mention the times when I would wander out onto the railroad tracks in Michigan or stand on the edge of Route 31 and think: *one step and it is over*. But love does not allow for easy exits. Even when everyone you love is gone. The wires pull hard at the chest. And you hang there suspended like a sideshow freak at the fair. Held upward by hooks in the skin, dangling. I say nothing. I nod. I promised Susan I would never read those journals. That I would burn them. I can remember the conversation, sitting in the house in Georgia. I didn't like morbid talk, but even in the first weeks of our marriage, Susan would speak of her death and what I should do should she die before me.

"If you want you can keep them for Cyrus and Darius, but only them."

But her parents got to the house before I could, while I lay half buried in a morphine stupor in Mass general; and they took everything from the home that held a memory of her. And those twenty bound journals must have seemed some great treasure trove. For a moment, it must have seemed they were holding their daughter. But of course they weren't. In the end what they found was paper and cardboard and ink. And words not meant to be read by anyone. If anything, those journals were a trove for Susan to dig through for poems and essays—to shape and form into something palpable and alive. Once in a while she would read a passage out loud if it was funny or sounded like the beginning of something she could turn to art. But I would keep my promise—both to her and to myself. I've lived enough pain in these past years to last anyone a lifetime. And now my in-laws must suffer as I suffer— the anger and guilt of every cross thought, every dark whim. And perhaps the upsweeping joy—

finding a mention of love, a happy memory of child-hood—only to lead to deeper troughs. They ride those winds—with the blind anger they have for the man who hurt their daughter, loved her, made love to her, nearly drove her to suicide, then had the gall to outlive her. So the most my mother-in-law will get is the blood coming up and flooding my neck and face—a change in breathing. Perhaps some sweat. And of course, hours of sleep lost.

* * *

On the Sabbath day I took my sons on walks through the city.

By then I had started keeping my own journal. In it, I would set down observations, anecdotes. The titles read like pages out of Thoreau's *Walden*—*On Labor, On Difference, Translation, Rubble*:

Amman's rubble is different. Or perhaps indifferent. There is no sediment, very little garbage, almost no twisted steelwork or piping. Just tons of crushed and piled limestone with tufted grass and scrub trees growing up through it. And there is no great effort being made at reconstruction—as if the broken, brittle lots are exactly what was planned for. Where construction progresses, it progresses slowly, at night, so the buildings and bridges seem to grow of their own accord rather than piece together mechanically. On a bright day, the jagged edges of stone light up and the heaps are as bright as any of the new buildings that surround them. Were these once houses, bridges, walls? Without the human story left behind in broken machines and furniture, even the occasional personal item as small as a bent spoon, it is hard to tell.

* * *

As a boy, I would take long walks though a field behind my house, leading past the water tanks and fish ponds to the distant tree line. There, just beyond the forest's edge was a square, ten-foot stone foundation halfway filled with dirt and pine-needles. On humid summer days I would go there and dig in the cool black loam for artifacts—some sign of what the building had been and who had lived there. I never found anything left by human hands beneath the forest floor. But the wind booming across the field and threading into the trees brought other treasures, caught in the depression as if in a lobster trap: a bright red ball, bags blown from the nearby grocery mart, a dollar bill, and once, the bones of a small bird, thin as lace and bleached with wind.

"What we want to be sure of," my father-in-law says, his face becoming solemn, stern, darkening, "is Susie's legacy. She worked very hard, you know, too hard, to just let it slip away." I have just told them about Rachael. And I'm a more than a little stunned. My father-in-law has hardly paused before moving on to other matters. I am always amazed at the emotional speed of our conversations. Love, Hate, Suicide, Rachael, Legacy. I hadn't been keeping it from them, but I hadn't told them either. Of course they knew. But how much? How much did Susie know? There is a longer story that they've only guessed at. I don't tell them how many years I had spent sleeping in a different room because I couldn't stand to love someone and not be allowed to touch her. Or the bizarre push and pull of affection and bitterness.

"Why are you still with me?" I once asked Susan.

"History has to mean something," she responded, her beautiful, tragic face in her hands.

The structure that was our marriage had collapsed on top of us, but there was no clear exit. No way out of the rubble, it seemed. I don't mention the long, hot walks with Rachael. The stolen whispers and cigarettes under the awnings of the creaking antebellum houses of Milledgeville. The late-night calls from pay phones at gas stations—just to have someone to talk to when things got desperate. When I felt shut in a deep box buried in the ground and looked for any light. The terrible panic of falling in love with the wrong person—or realizing I was with the wrong person all along, ten years into a marriage. The strange mix of anger and hope I felt as Rachael began to confide more and more of her terror, her own desperation. Even if I were to explain it all I couldn't begin. It came. It was beyond me. And it scared me to death. A month into therapy, my therapist looked at me hard and said, "Tell me about Rachael," when I thought I had been talking only of her each day every day.

"No, you talk about your marriage, Susan, Cyrus sometimes, but not often." "Avoidance," she said. "We still have a lot of work to do."

And I knew she was right. But Rachael was still with her abuser—a man who still called me to ask for advice about writing, about love. And I had to pretend I didn't know who he really was or what he did. I had to pretend I liked him because Rachael begged me to. Because he wanted to "throw his arms around me and make me promise to be his friend forever," when he disgusted me more than anyone I'd ever known by then. Avoidance. I'm still doing it. But how? Where to start? Rachael made the world shatter and come together again in new combinations just by walking across a road before me and almost tipping over with the awkward grace of a failed and faltering prima ballerina—at once exquisite and vulnerable. She still compares herself to Susan, but I don't; I never did. What I loved in Rachael were the contradictions: the innocent pout, the arched eyebrow, the easy tears, and the sharp retort. But these are abstractions. Is it enough to say that Rachael was the first person I've ever really collapsed in front of? Just collapsed, like someone pulled the last pillar of support from a condemned building. Or maybe it only takes one pillar to fall, to take the weight of all those accumulated moments— all that history: a baby being born blue and silent, then screaming all at once, the first shared poem, a photograph of two skiers on a mountaintop in France, the cramped storage space beneath an apartment in Lincoln, Nebraska. And the pillars falling; myself, Susan. Rachael asking, "why don't you just leave?"

And all I could do was stare and think of the ocean I stood by as a boy, and the sand cliffs and the houses peeking over, destined to fall as the sand eroded beneath them, and the light coming at me on the water, angry and roaring. Avoidance. Delicate shoulders, slim, graceful neck, the line of a chin. How badly I wanted to feel that again for Susan, but couldn't; how quickly there was only Rachael.

How far could it have gone, I often wonder, had we not left for Jordan on Fulbrights? For a long time, lying in bed in one hospital then another, I wondered if my love for Rachael had been the push that set the tragedy in motion. Where does it start? We dig and dig for cause—the origins of things. But I know that beginnings, like endings, stretch off in both directions forever and we are destined to live our lives and deaths *in medias res* with all the lack of purpose and confusion that entails.

I could answer my father-in-law this way— explaining that I have begun the process of sifting through Susie's work, trying to pick up the threads of her projects. But so many of them evade me. We did not speak much in the last months and had different friends. Lived different lives in separate rooms—two caged birds; her, the peacock searching for a garden, and me, a flightless heron, a hawk, some gull, a bird of garbage, winged and wounded. Still, I have done what I can, pieced together a manuscript and sent it to her publisher, gone through the boxes and tried to make sense of projects half-completed. And every word is a sting. Every line a twist of the knife.

* * *

The only artifacts are those blown around the city in the desert sand and windstorms that come once or twice a month, sending garbage bags, sheets, and clothes off the lines—anything not spiked, roped or nailed to earth— into the air to be snagged in the rubble for the play and scavenging of stray cats. The urge to join them in their dig among the detritus is powerful. But I don't believe it would yield any discoveries. It's as if before each building was leveled, the levelers had picked it clean of all human record.

Even in a journal entry I could not be completely honest. Even when the audience is the self—one can fear its rejection, its revulsion. And I had grown disgusted with myself. For years I couldn't even look in the mirror without wanting to spit at my reflection. Sometimes I did. I've learned how hard it is to revisit the past honestly or see the present fully even

when, especially when, the only real judge is looking back at you over a bathroom sink. So much lay
beneath the lines. It was mere travelogue. And the
traveler was moving from one place to another without real contact, accumulating none of the stains of
intimacy, floating really, like a plastic bag hopping
over stones, parked cars, waiting for a tree branch
to catch it for a while. Those words seem so unreal
now—so detached and elegant. Of course, it was all
fresh paint over rotten planks.

*In a telephone conversation, a close friend suggested
that this rubble could serve as a fit metaphor for the
soul. A poetic idea. But I think it more likely represents
the soul's ruins, how hard it is to dig past them. An old
man's face, like that of the taxi driver Ali with his military fatigues and smoldering cigar, is equally ruined—
sun-scarred and pocked with insult—both physical and
emotional. Perhaps suggested in those lines there is some
great regret or anger, a distant lover, a lost child, a stolen
home, shame and humiliation personal and cultural. But
the truth is hidden from us beneath this human rubble.*

Only a man obsessed with love could imagine a
lover for Ali. And of course, I knew it was fantasy.
Projection. I was thinking of Rachael, who stopped
my heart merely by almost falling over while cross-

ing a street. And the truth was not hidden. It was frightening. What if I left Susan? What if she finally left me? What then? Did Rachael feel this way for me? Or was she merely an imagined beam of light in the rubble? The mind searching desperately for hope. And what of the children, where are they in these notes to the self? How desperately I would like to read a description of Cyrus now that he is gone. Where are you, my beautiful boy? Pushed from behind by the hands of a man who isn't really there.

* * *

"I love you more than anybody," Darius shouts from the back of the car as I weave through the traffic of Hartford, Connecticut. He has spent another two weeks with Susan's parents and he is still glowing with reunion. Tonight he will cry for his Bibi. Tomorrow he will ask if we can call his mother and brother. And when I say no, they are in heaven, he'll pretend he didn't ask, giving an awkward smile and turning his attention back to his coloring book.

"Darius, you don't have to love me more than everybody. You can love us all differently."

"But I love you best."

"But you don't have to, you know. For Bibi you can have Bibi-Love. For me, Daddy-Love. For Rachael, Rachael-Love. And Mommy-love. And Cyrus-love." He starts to giggle, and I point at our golden retriever, Jack-Jack in the passenger seat. "Even doggy-love."

Now he is laughing really hard, squirming in his car seat, shouting "Doggy-love. Jack-Jack-love!" "It's the same for me. I love Rachael, and I love you, and I love Jack-Jack. But I don't love any of you in the same way."

"Do you love Rachael more than Mommy?"

Mommy.

Sitting on the colorful carpets of our sitting room in our massive cold apartment in Amman, brochures spread around her, Susan, cell phone in one hand, personal organizer in another, was a picture of the determined traveler: bright, efficient, and ready to go. We were making our first excursion beyond the borders of the city to Jarash and she glowed with the prospect of adventure. To be honest, I wasn't that enthusiastic. I was excited to see the Roman ruins but the expedition seemed touristy. I imagined myself walking behind a smiling, head-bobbing, guide, eager to show me everything I wanted to see and tell me everything I wanted to know, catering to my every wish and charging me for every second of it. I've never liked tour guides—in any country. No matter how well they treat you, you know the experience is false. That human being is reduced to his function, which is to please, and you are reduced to commerce. You stop being Joel or Susan or Cyrus and become ten dollars, francs, pounds or dinars.

Still it was an easy sell; the brochures written in Arabic, French, German, and English with bright photographs of columns marching into pale blue sky were more than I could resist. I've always believed that ruins have a special pull to the American, for whom an old city was founded two hundred, not two thousand, years ago. Where there are no ancient castles in the midst of its cities, no temples from long abandoned religions—where what is ancient in our land is only beginning to be excavated in the western prairies and deserts, and our sense of self is based more on faith and system than by tradition. Separated from the ancient civilizations not only by time but oceans, the possibility of actually traveling to an ancient city is as remote to most of us as a trip to Mars, and just as alluring.

More than that, there was something personal.
If ever I had been lost in my life, I was lost then, and
no matter how hard I tried to focus on the moment,
I could not look at this beautiful talented woman
without thinking of all that I had lost, was losing
each day. And to look at Susan was to fall in love
with her. She had an undeniable beauty, not only
of body—with her long black hair, dark almond-
shaped eyes and teardrop chin—but of spirit. Susie
emanated. I've never been sure what exactly. But she
emanated. Her presence literally seemed to push out
the air around her. And this presence was compel-
ling and isolating. It pulled people to her, but kept
them from ever really getting to understand her
deeply. The previous night we had had one of those
brutal arguments that you know will follow you for
the rest of your marriage. We were hired to teach
American Literature and Creative Writing. But of
course, at the University of Amman, there were only
a few course offerings in those areas and most were
taught by senior faculty. And Susie wanted them.
The truth was, she didn't want to teach at all. She
wanted to write. And her experiences talking to the
Palestinian refugees had galvanized her. She wanted
to write of them, for them. And she wasn't going

to spend her time preparing lessons on seventeenth century British Literature. At first I acquiesced. Susie had a way of making her position sound not only like the most reasonable one, but the only one.

"It would be easier for you, Joel; you are a scholar, after all. You can learn anything, teach anything. You're brilliant."

She was good at appealing to my vanity. But I knew I was being manipulated.

"Susie, look; this isn't fair. You must see that."

Then her expression darkened as it always did when she felt accused of a breach in ethics or morals.

"Don't talk to me about fair." And then, "I gave up my life for you. You wouldn't even be here if it weren't for me."

There was little I could say. As usual, a minor disagreement had exploded into something far beyond its scope. She was right. Whatever my accomplishments as a scholar and a teacher, it was her work as an Iranian-American poet and National Poetry Series winner that made us attractive to the Fulbright people. But it was the statement, "I gave up my life for you," words that had become a sad refrain over the previous years, that lingered. I know that Susie believed this. Her marriage to me was what locked her to the United States. It was what lost her Swiss citizenship; it was what kept her from visiting Iran; it was a sacrifice I could never repay, and one which placed our relationship in such disharmony and imbalance that nothing in our marriage existed without its permeating vapor. And then I did something that still makes me shudder. I closed my eyes to her beautiful mouth and chin and pleading hands;

"You cruel, cold, bitch."

And the door slammed shut.

Perhaps that night, Susan wrote in her journal that she would leave me. I wouldn't blame her. Perhaps she wrote down her hatred for me. At my worst moments, I deserved it. Susie was never cold—when she finally retreated from me, it was not from a lack of passion, but, I think, too much. We used each other up and quickly. The way a fire makes quick work of old wooden buildings in a market square. We were both exhausted. Literally burned and hollowed out by it all. By the massive *effort* it all took. But there we were, caged together by hatred and love and children, and that huge weight that had built up on top of us, of harsh words and poetry, and all that stretching to meet halfway when the distance between us had always been oceanic—as broad and churning as history itself. And history meant something, after all.

* * *

Though not very clean, the bus ride to Jarash is quick (forty-five minutes total) and comfortable. The busses are small, like oversized versions of the torpedo-tube VW van my father used to own and drive all over the country—though dad's bus didn't have burgundy, tassled drapes hanging from the windows, or an old woman fingering torquise prayer beads while draped in a hajab of black and gold cotton. The outlying hills of Amman offer a stark contrast to the bustling, industrial streets of the city, with its towering deluxe hotels and extensive markets. Out in the pastures and orchards life is lived closer to the land. The squat, limestone houses, do not so much nestle into the hillsides as cling to them as if they could, any moment, be picked up by the wind and blown away. And this seems deliberate. Few trees rise above seven feet and most are bent toward the earth as if in prayer. The ones that venture upward are thin, conical firs that resemble a too-skinny girl's arms thrust into clear quick,

water; awkward and graceful at the same moment.
Towns dot the landscape and seem to blend into the
farmland. Here a young girl in a blue fleece pullover leans against the dusty wall of a gas station, a
mural of Rambo over her head; here two boys chase
each other, playing some form of violent tag beneath
and around a gigantic diesel tank, suspended in the
air by chains tied to metal girders; here a girl in a
pink pullover skips down a hillside and throws her
arms around a mountain goat. On the side of the
highway, a shepherd guides a flock of thirty dusty
but obedient sheep toward better grazing on some
distant plateau.

The hills themselves are rolling and golden
brown, speckled with white limestone boulders and
green grass, or fruit trees. Occasionally, in the deep-
est valleys, a small lake shines. I find myself comparing the landscape to the red dirt of Georgia, or
Virginia. And just before reaching the city, passing
through the highways cut most deeply through the
mountains, the dynamite-blasted limestone passages
remind me of similar roads torn through the hills of
Vermont and Massachusetts. We carry our worlds
with us wherever we go.

But we don't necessarily reveal them. With my blond hair, blue eyes, and blue jeans, I was as obviously American as a can of Coca-Cola or the Nike swoosh. As a result, I was a magnet for the searching eyes and broken English of those Jordanians as curious about my country as I was about theirs. And at that time, I so desperately wanted to blend in somewhere, somehow. A part of me was always afraid—not of being targeted as an American but as a hypocrite. And if a pair of dark eyes looked too deeply, I always wondered, "Can they tell? Can they see who I am?" I had thrown a pearl to the sea, after all, and I knew it and felt the regret of it, but at the same time I couldn't stop thinking of Rachael. She grew up on a farm, I thought, staring at the small farms blurring into the landscape as the bus picked up speed suicidally down the mountainsides—what kind of farm? And I thought of the essay she read about pig busses—converted yellow school busses filled with pigs—rolling through the cornfields of Michigan. I stared hard out the glass, away from Susan, away from any potential searching eyes.

There was little need. Susie was with Darius in another aisle. And on the bus, I was left alone. In my pocket of silence, staring out the window with Cyrus propped against my shoulder, drifting in and out of sleep, I seemed of little interest to any of my fellow travelers—another passenger among passengers. To people splitting their lives between city and suburb on their way to work, or to visit a loved one, a lone tourist, whatever his appearance or nationality, seemed of no consequence.

But everything was of consequence to me— the foreigner, tourist, scholar, father, husband. Everything new and old at once. Everything charged with the shock of similarity—some moment, some tree or valley, some expression called up from childhood. Everything charged with the shock of difference and distance, with how far away I was, how uncertain the ground beneath me. And how weak the rattling roof above. Each breath seemed to take concentration. And when I wasn't floating above the land beneath my feet or totally walled off from the world around me, I was so raw from feeling that at times I imagined I'd been flayed alive. That I walked through wind and rain and sandstorm without any skin at all. There were times when I could barely look at my children—especially Cyrus, with his wisp of a body, ghost-like skin, and eyes so

dark they seemed all pupil, as if he were always staring wide-eyed into darkness. *He knows*, I'd think. I
still do sometimes. What must it have been like for
him—caught between adults traveling at high speed
in opposite directions with him in the middle—each
of us overcompensating like crazy. Smothering him
with overtight embraces.

* * *

*By the time the columns of Jarash (Garazia to the
Romans) loomed on the horizon, I was already worn out.*

*Thankfully, we were spared the necessity of a tour
guide when we met a computer science teacher in a
local high school named Akmed, a Palestinian who took
us under his wing, first marching us to the best place
to get hummus and kabob and then guiding us through
the ancient ruins. Later, over coffee at our apartment
during a break from Arabic lessons, Akmed told us that
it was God who noticed us on the bus, God who made
him see that we needed help, and God, in the guise of
my mother-in-law, who made us see that he would be a
good teacher.*

My mother-in-law, of course, loved this. And
immediately loved Akmed. As did we all. And
though she was constantly comparing Jordan to her

native Iran—at Jordan's disadvantage—she loved Jordan, too. It was not her home, but it was her element. She spoke no Arabic, but she could communicate with these people, mixing English, French, Farsi, and hand signals dramatically to make a point, learning words and laughing off misunderstanding. And with Akmed there was recognition. They understood each other. None of us were suspicious of him. And we had no reason to be. He was a beautiful and spiritual man. One of the few true men of God I have met in my life. My mother-in-law convinced him not only to guide us around Jarash that day, but to teach us Arabic three nights a week. I've forgotten almost all of it now. But I remember him, the thin brown coat that seemed to be rotting around him, the constant five-o'clock shadow, the tar-blackened fingertips, the way he would lean over my shoulder, breathing in my ear as I strained with effort, then leap up, celebrate, when I would get a word or concept right. *He study. He study. Al hamdel Allah. Al hamdel Allah.*

Thanks God, Akmed said. And God may have been at work. I don't know. If we hadn't met Akmed that day, Susie and Cyrus would most certainly still be alive right now. We would not have been in his friend's van traveling to Aqaba on the Sabbath day; we wouldn't have placed our lives first in his hands, then the sleepy-eyed driver's, then God's, on an unlit desert highway. We wouldn't have hit that sand truck. Akmed would be alive too. I wouldn't be a single father writing forlorn essays in a two-bedroom apartment on the side of a mountain in New Hampshire. And I wouldn't be with Rachael now. *Al hamdel Allah. Al hamdel Allah.* How the ironies accumulate. How my life has become this convoluted mix of suffering and hope. My father-in-law says he doesn't know if he believes in God anymore. For a long time he would sit on the couch in his family room, not sleeping, trying to figure out a way that someone was responsible for it all as the news droned on behind him. As the world refused to stop even a moment in its revolutions. It was a "hit," he said once, that Akmed was really a terrorist and Susie, as a writer of controversial poetry, was a target of the Iranian government or some branch of Al Quaida or the Israeli Secret Service. The banality of accidents is more than anyone can take. Accidents are meaningless, pointless, and brutally real. What was that sand truck *doing* across the road at that moment on that day? (Clearing sand.) And who was this driver, this man with the droopy eyes who my mother-in-law now swears was on opium? (Just a friend of Akmed's, picking up presents in Aqaba for his wife and kids.) And Akmed. How well did we really know this Akmed anyway? (He taught computers in a Palestinian neighborhood for a school that had only two computers for two hundred students.)

My mother-in-law is mostly silent on the matter of God. She writes poetry now—tells Darius she is writing a book for him. Like me, trying to understand it all, make something of it all. Not so much accept it, but make events spin and turn and change to what she would make them. An epic story with heroes and villains. And I find the poems beautiful. Tragic in what they try to do, in what they represent, as much as what they are. There is recognition. I understand these people. Even if we don't communicate as well as we'd like, even when the simplest disagreement erupts into the ugliest of arguments. There was a time when I was always looking into the essence of things. Years ago, a poet friend of mine returned a manuscript with just a few words scrawled on it: *Joel, I worry about you; you are always almost desperately searching out the meaning of things. But not everything is meaningful. Most things just are.*

I took it as an unintentional compliment. I am not glib. I am not clever, I thought; I am passionate—intense. And I still believe in essences, in the soul. But I guess I have become less determined to understand them, more willing to accept that some knowledge is not mine to have. I believe in God more than ever. But I don't know why.

Avoidance?

Perhaps I believe because I have to. Because I survived. And there must be a reason. But to believe that would be to believe that there was purpose too in a young boy flying through shattered glass at seventy miles an hour on a cold night in a desert. "I can't believe in a God who would let this happen," my father-in-law says, and I feel myself thinking, "Neither could I."

Now my mother-in-law sits across me, and I honestly don't know what she feels as I tell her that Rachael and I are together. That we love each other. That we are happy. I want to say, "You don't understand. The building had collapsed, you see. There was no light. I was buried in it."

Heroes and villains. Poetry.

Al hamdel Allah. Al hamdel Allah.

* * *

Under Akmed's more certain gaze, following behind in the path of his relaxed gate and the vapor trail of his always-burning cigarette, we moved through the gates of the ancient city. I'd not expected the ruins to be so complete or large. Two gigantic theatres were almost perfectly intact and I was able to climb to the top, boys in tow, and sit in the cheap seats, imagining what entertainment went on down below. The Oval Plaza was also intact and one could still see the grooves worn in the roads by chariots and carts. The two temples to Artemis were in worse shape, nearly flattened both by earthquakes and by the desecration visited upon them by Christians in later centuries. It was exhilarating to stand and sit in places that were once the center of commerce, trade, and art for centuries, to look down the columned thoroughfares and wonder how busy they once were. But it was also overwhelming. Leaning on a wall in what was once the inner chamber of the temple of Artemis, I couldn't help but wonder what men and women labored and hoped and prayed here, what rituals they performed to give contour and meaning to their lives. Again I was struck with an almost desperate longing, trying to repopulate the city, filling the lonely market square with men and women like those I'd seen in the "suq" on the other side of the highway—shouting, laughing, and struggling, a certain desperation behind each barter, each lowering of price. A woman with blackened hands sews a pair of shoes, another pulls the hand of a small child as it screams and laughs; two men shout over the price of perfume, or the hind end of a lamb. What scents of spices and burning fuel made the air shimmer? What colors and clothes did they wear? Did they love and hate each other? Were their desperations like mine? And if they could stare across history to meet my gaze would there be recognition— and would that recognition comfort or horrify? Would I still avert my eyes?

From my vantage point on the ruined temple mount I could see Susie and Akmed in the distance. Akmed was standing thirty feet above the ground on the ledge of a stone tower and was waving Susie over. Bending at the waist, open hand turned up, as if asking for a waltz. She hugged her arms around her, shook her head and laughed; that bright, sharp, wind chime laughter. I cannot honestly recreate what I felt just then.

Avoidance.
Jealousy.
Love.
Fear.
Exhilaration.
Regret.
Longing.
My mother-in-law remembers this moment, too. And offers it up as evidence of some sinister intent on the part of Akmed. But I don't think she believes it. Because when you meet a good man in this world, you know it. And Akmed was simply and beautifully good. And if he was reckless then, he was reckless like a man who has discovered the reality of God and finds in that belief no answers, just some powerful creative presence that may or may not be just or kind. Whose ways are foreign to us and whose powers beyond our understanding. And so he dances on the ruins, thankful for his little life, his little death.

* * *

And I wonder, did they love or hate their emperor, that lonely foreigner in whose name the taxes were levied and temples built? And when Hadrian at last made his one visit and viewed the great arch constructed in his honor, did he feel as if he knew these people, did he care to? Or did this city blur and blend, as cities must, to an emperor, something to hold in his worldly hand and toss in the air like a ball?

That arch, finished just before his arrival, was to stand as the new gate to the city. But the gate was never finished. And still, it stands a lonely sentry to the city in the distance. After thousands of years as one of the hubs of commerce in the Middle East, the trade routes changed and very gradually, Garazia became depopulated, fell into ruin, and was covered in sand, where it remained preserved in obscurity until a German traveler recognized the ruins. Eighty years later, archeologists are still uncovering the remnants of this ancient and mysterious world.

We spent many hours walking through Garazia before hiring a van to take us back (the next bus was a good thirty minutes off and the children were exhausted by then). Driving back, I nodded off to sleep as our new teacher began his lessons, reciting the names of towns and cities. One of them, where I had seen the two boys playing beneath the fuel tank, was originally a Palestinian refugee camp. Now it's squat houses spread out for miles, the land swelling with their descendents. I was struck, as usual, by the enormity of what I still don't know about this country, about the world. Akmed smiled, guiding me through it as best as he could, taking me home to other journeys, other, more lonely excavations.

Such is the work of the archeologist of the city and the city's soul. Where we are always pulled along as much by mystery as beauty. And rubble is merely a name for traces left by human hands and loss and time.

Resisting Elegy

We are at another reception for the annual writer's convention. In the past ten years I have only missed one of these—the year of the accident. And it's hard being here. So many times Susan would stand at the center of the crowd dressed in red velour or silk. She was beautiful in red. And the enchanted revelers would orbit around her. It is a different year and I am with a different woman. And I know it must seem obscene to some people, seeing me here, happy and laughing. I am doing the best I can. Rachael's mellifluous laughter chimes behind me somewhere and I am desperate to drift into it, merge with it. Or to pull her from the room and run. Or simply make a break for the door by myself, a movie gangster, gun in the air, daring someone to raise his head from the floor or call the cops. I imagine the scene—well-tailored suit, fedora pulled low, "Nobody moves and nobody gets hurt." I always look good in my fantasies, full of charm, charisma, and a brooding, feral appeal; hard-hearted and strong. But in real life I am too often uncertain, ready to weep at any moment and easily hurt. And I am a poor actor. Always searching for my sea legs as the ground shifts beneath me. At least these are the metaphors I mix with a plastic cup of *Maker's Mark* and ice as I stare at this man I don't know and try to formulate an intelligible phrase—something sympathetic and kind and suitably sad. But he has already seen me laughing and drunk, obviously happy—not what he expected at all. He tells me that he loved Susan's work and has a dog-eared copy of her book by his bedside. As has happened too many times, I am faced again with the concerned, mildly confused, vaguely disappointed faces of the belatedly grieving. The next introduction is perfunctory: Marty, a friend and colleague of Susan's from her last job at a college in Georgia, walks over two young women who want to meet me—he passes them to me with all the ceremony of a father leaving his daughter at the altar. And looks over his shoulder as he leaves, surveying the scene, waiting for something to happen. I don't blame Marty. I don't blame these young writers. I don't blame anyone. A few years seems such a short time to someone who hasn't lived it each day—hasn't endured the silences of an empty room, alive with absence and accusation. Or hasn't wrapped an arm around a lover so broken with grief and regret by a photograph slipping from a book that he can't stand up or breathe. What they want is so simple, what Marty wants, what every romantic onlooker wants—a grieving husband who can pass a memory to add to the shrine they wish to build. It occurs to me that they don't ask about Cyrus, the son who also died in the car accident. Nor do they ask of Darius, the boy I now raise on my own. Perhaps they don't know this part of the story. Perhaps it doesn't matter to them. Almost no one ever asks or says anything about the boys—an irony particularly bitter when I remember how much the boys were the center of Susan's life and thought. "Thank you," I say, mouthing the words. And . . . nothing comes. I have nothing to give them.

I have tried many times to do it. I understand the anger, the outrage. It is such a small concession to pretend, really. To play the broken widower. To write that beautiful memorial for the review. To give a speech to satisfy an audience at the award to be presented in her name. Even Rachael feels it, when I answer the concerned and gentle questioner,

"Actually we are doing really well. Darius is a little miracle. I'm blessed with so much. And of course, Rachael, too. We're happy."

"You don't have to say that, you know," Rachael says, resting a hand on mine, quietly. "You don't have to tell them that everything is fine." What she means is, "I've been there. I've seen. Don't pretend." So why, then? What do I get from rejecting the offer to grieve with them at any moment the need arises? Why not give them just a little? Acknowledge that I suffer and let them be satisfied? Open up the wallet and show them not only the picture of Darius, but Cyrus and Susan on that last day, bathing knee-deep in the Red Sea outside of Aqaba. And cry for God's sake.

And it would not all be pretense. I loved her. Love her still. And she was beautiful. I could distill the best of her. And isn't that what we most deserve? When Polonius says that he will treat the players "according to their desert," Hamlet replies, "better: use every man after his desert and who should scape the whipping?"

* * *

An attempt:

We are at the apartment just after Cyrus's birth. It's late August, 1998, and the air conditioner is working overtime. I have never changed a diaper before and Susan can't help. A Caesarian scar runs across her lower abdomen. For years she will tell me that it hurts her when she laughs or when it is tapped or touched in just the wrong manner. How it feels like the skin of a drum—some aching hollowness beneath. I strap the little belly down as Cyrus screams. His little penis seems red and sore and as I stare down at it, he starts to pee, a little fountain arcing up and back, splashing on his belly.

"Oops." I place my hand over it as I search for a wipe or a towel.

Susie is making little breathy sounds behind me, saying, "Please, don't make me laugh, I'll tear right open." At this point, I'm thinking, what the hell is funny about this? The fountain stops, and Cyrus's scream turns to a little giggle, a toothless smile. Susie is doubled over behind me, sinking to the floor.

"Oh, you think that's funny, huh?" And I start to smile. Then his face changes, the eyes knitting together as if deep in concentration.

When I see the large brown circle on the wall two feet behind us, formed after a single large blast, my first thought is, "Wow. Impressive. I didn't know they could do that." Then, "Thank God I was out of the line of fire." Susie is rolling and twisting on the floor now in her white nightgown, alternating between moans of pain and laughter. Cyrus is screaming again. Even as I wipe at the now off-white wall with a moist wet sponge, I feel good. Whole. We are a family. Like everyone else.

"Honey," I say, as she nurses him, "I never thought fatherhood would mean cleaning my son's shit off a wall."

* * *

I can almost feel the gentle hands touching my shoulders as I write this. *That's it,* they say. *That wasn't so bad, was it? Keep going. Remember, this is a eulogy. What does it all mean? Go on. You're doing great.*

And so.

And that was Susie . . .

But it isn't and wasn't. I'm not even certain that it was her story. Just an anecdote from when we were happy. Scene. Commentary. Scene. And I'm supposed to make sense of it. What kind of eulogy has shit on the wall, anyway. I'm no good at this.

* * *

Attempt number 2:

We are in a canoe on East Lake in Oakland, Maine. It is our first summer together after the honeymoon, working at a boy's camp—Susie as a photographer, me as a baseball coach. We have placed an old door over the canoe and a towel on top of that so Susie can lie out in the sun while I paddle. Her olive skin oiled, her night-black hair fanned beneath her head, massive tortoise-shell sunglasses hiding her eyes, she looks like a beauty from a James Bond film, waiting for Roger or Sean to make a pass, so she might icily brush it aside. "Look," my father says, pointing from the dock. "Cleopatra's Barge." Susie and I laugh. Yes, it's ridiculous, but I enjoy this kind of play. Already we are doing it far less often. The camp has not been a good experience for us. Our cabin is cold and wet in rainy weather and hot and stifling in the heat. We must retreat to the lake or under blankets or into my car for long drives among the back roads for relief, Susie drifting off to sleep as I sing Blues Traveler's "The Hook Brings You Back" at the top of my lungs. We hardly talk any longer—afraid perhaps, of what the other would have to say. I practically grew up in this place, attending every summer of my childhood, and I had hoped that bringing Susie there would bring us closer together. But we worked best as a couple in isolation—no families or parents or colleagues to take sides or pull us apart. So we find ways to literally paddle off.

Every once in a while she lifts her head to comment on the way my shoulders and back move as I paddle, then lifts her sunglasses to wink and smile. Occasionally a loon slips up from the water, a long silhouette in the early evening sunlight. Then just as quickly, is gone again. We glide along, away from shore, and for a while, and for once, life seems easy, something that could be ridden and slipped along with long, smooth strokes, not fought against or through—until the wind picks up.

At first it is nothing, just a few gusts blowing the heat from our bodies, offering relief. But the weather changes fast on the water and soon the wind is blowing the light aluminum canoe sideways and then in circles. I can't control it. The course I took in water safety when I was thirteen years old seems no help at all. Before long we are hopelessly stranded among some rocks behind the shelter of a small island. I am swearing and screaming and thrashing at the water with a paddle. At least thirty gulls that would have normally scattered at the approach of a boat stand on the rocks, hunched against the wind, ignoring us. And we hunch with them for a moment. Just two more members of the flock. One, perched just a few feet away, seems to stare at my fury with a studied and mildly amused cock of the head. Susie notices. Stares at me. Stares at the bird. Stares back at me.

"Yeah, I know what you're thinking," she says to the perturbed gull. "What the fuck is wrong with him?"

* * *

But this is no help at all. As my mother-in-law told me after reading a copy of my first essay about the accident and its aftermath, I "didn't do it right." Susie hardly talks, playing a bit part at best. And again, it makes references to our problems as a couple, however vague. And the tone. The tone is all wrong.

Believe it or not, I really am doing my best. But I admit it is the work of exhaustion, not of will. There is a moment at the end of Arthur Miller's *The Crucible* when the Reverend Hale begs Proctor to sign a confession for wizardry. All he must do is sign his name and he will be saved—a mere act of repentance and contrition. And it is not as if he hasn't sinned. Who is he—adulterer, liar that he is—who is he to stand on ethics, to say, "It is my name," when signing would save him, would save others the pain of his death, the pain of the guilt his death would bring? It may not have been *his* sin, exactly, but it was sin. I imagine the force of pressure bearing in on him as he puts the pen to the paper. *I've confessed already*, he thinks. So why not this? Because it is a lie? What justifications go through a man's mind at that moment? Is one crime the same as another?

And it isn't a lie, I tell myself. It's merely selection. No more a lie than anything I've written. And isn't art always a process of selection? A beautiful shell game, smoke and mirrors. Nothing up my sleeve. The gunman waves his pistol in the air to make the victim stare at the gun, not the man who holds it. Look where I tell you to look. The gun commits the crime and not the man. And you can't see what's not there, can you? Nobody moves, nobody gets hurt. And if you keep your head down and count to ten, I'll be gone.

I lift the pen from the paper. The trapdoor releases at my feet.

* * *

I hold a photograph up to my students and ask, "is this true?" They stare back, questioning. They know I'm playing with them. "It's a photograph," Robert says.

"But is it true?"

"How could it be a lie?" Alec asks.

"Because it only shows part of the picture. We can't see what's on the edges of the frame."

"If it's a good photograph, then its true," Emily, an art student, interjects.

"But what is a bad photograph really—one that makes us look bad or one that tells the wrong story?"

"But how can you tell the wrong story? How can a story be wrong? I mean it's the photographer's story, right?"

"You can't put *everything* in the picture."

"Exactly. All art is, at least in part, about what gets left in and what gets left out of the frame."

"So is a story a lie if it leaves out something important?"

"No, sometimes those are the most powerful stories. The ones that hint at more than what they show."

Alec raises his hand, frustrated. "But it's not a story; it's a photograph."

"Are you saying that all art is a lie? That artists are liars?"

"No."

* * *

In the digital, sepia-toned photograph taken in spring 2003 on Tybee Island, Georgia, the horizon line is razor sharp—ocean dark and brooding gray-brown, the sky the color of fine sand. At foreground, my sons play: Cyrus, prone, his suit hung low below the tan line, his bottom the same fine-sand brightness of the sky. Darius, nearly round, plays with him. Does he remember any of this? When he is older, will he wonder, as I wonder, *What was I thinking then? What exactly did I see? How did I feel, if I felt anything?* And what of the photographer, Susan, buffeted by the same wind that tosses the boys' black hair so that to take the shot she must keep brushing strands of it away. So much is left out of the picture, so much caught in the frame and kept as if the elements of the moment are on separate sides of a locked stable door that swings both out and in. And the watcher reaches over it, the animal starts, backing off, skittish, powerful and out of reach.

A few months after the accident, I took Darius to a child therapist. After watching him play on the floor with blocks and some small plastic animals, the therapist told me, to my surprise, that my son was doing fine. That he had created a peaceable kingdom. No violence or war. When he created a pen for the animals, he did not block it. And he let them come and go and move about freely. "He's in the arms of love," the man said. And I was relieved to hear it. "But what do I tell him," I asked. "How do I tell him about his mother and brother?"

"He will tell you, I suspect. He'll ask the questions and you will answer them the best that you can. What he remembers will be images. A face over a crib. A smell at dinner time. The sound of his brother's laughter. And it will be a while before he'll be able to articulate this. You'll need to be patient and affirming. Let him guide you. His mother will be a beautiful collage, created by everyone who knew her."

Images. Not stories. Questions, not answers. And of course the large gaps in between.

Like Darius, all I can bring together are moments, images. And they wheel around me, changing shape and form even as I try to put them down. They slip and run away from my grasp. I can't tell you what the defining moment was. I can't place you behind her eyes as she took the photograph. But I can tell you that she took it. And I can point to her paintings and say, she painted that. And her story is right there for us if we choose to see it. And Cyrus? I don't know. I keep drawing pictures in the sand and the winds and waves take them. I try to think the dust into starlings. But it stays dust, fiery with sunlight. I turn to Rachael and say, I miss my boy. I miss both of them. I hold the photograph in my hand, saying again and again: Cyrus. Susan. Cyrus. Susan. And pray for stillness. Please, nobody move. Nobody moves and nobody gets hurt.

PLEASE TAKE
WHAT YOU WANT
SEPTEMBER, 2007

THE BIKE WAS NOT the last thing to go. Back in the little apartment in the old brick dormitory on the hill, amid boxes and bubble wrap, sharpies and box cutters, there were still the odds and ends—things I didn't yet know what to do with and things that needed to be thrown out or given away—last minute decisions and indecisions. That, in the end, frantic with the passage of time, I would leave them on the stoop with a box-flap sign—*PLEASE TAKE WHAT YOU WANT*. It wasn't the first either. Even with my bad hip aching and my sciatic nerves firing in protest, I had managed to cart half my possessions down the switchback, rain-slicked utility road, just below the daycare playground. Chairs went, old appliances—the faux-cherry hutch that Susan and I bought weeks after we had moved into our first apartment in Lincoln, Nebraska—all of it was hefted and tossed over the edge of the dumpster, to ring hollow or splinter to pieces. I worked quickly, trying not to think too much, sweating and huffing under weight and awkwardness of weight, accumulating scratches and bruises. Sometimes the children would stare down at me, and I'd try not to look at them, not to make eye contact. One little girl from Darius's class stared for a long time as I hefted a large stuffed animal won years ago at a fair. Our eyes locked and her mouth moved. I don't know and didn't try to make out what she was saying, but I felt the blood come to my face and my strength go—as if I were in the process doing some shameful thing and she was witness to it.

I hadn't asked for help, though there would have been plenty of people willing to help. I was a popular teacher at this little school in New Hampshire— worshipped in little ways I never understood, nor was particularly comfortable with. To them, I was a survivor—some kind of emblem of strength in the face of tragedy. But I didn't feel strong and I didn't see anything admirable in simply being alive. In all those hopeful faces I couldn't find a single young man or woman from whom I wanted help. Perhaps I didn't want to implicate them in what I was doing—no reason to stain anyone else's hands. This life was mine to dispose of. Mine to throw away.

Two days earlier I had let two of my colleagues go with me to the storage facility where I kept most of the belongings I couldn't fit in my little apartment or couldn't bear to look at. The entire drive down the mountainside I stared directly at the road, not speaking. These were good guys, people who would have listened if I wanted them to, would have put a hand on my shoulder if I broke down over a box of Cyrus's artwork, an old wedding album, or the headboard of a marriage bed. But I don't remember saying much, other than *thank you*. I worked hard and fast. I even gave that headboard to one of them, Eric, who had just gotten married and was sleeping with his mattress on the floor. I offered it in an off-hand way that shocked him a little—*Do you think you could use this?* He must have asked me fifty times if I was sure—staring at me as if I had gone a little crazy. I was. I averted their eyes and tried not to wonder what they were looking for or at when they looked at me. And I promised myself that from then on, like some gun-slinging hero of the old west, I would work alone.

I've come to believe that my need to grieve in isolation has something to do with an awareness of audience. In an argumentation and persuasion

class that I now teach at a little community college in Ohio, I tell my students that in writing, the
imagined audience is nearly everything. What you
know of them, what you imagine them to be (farm-
ers, young working mothers, teachers and coaches,
a teenage girl who hates her parents)—their fears
and desires, their needs and hopes, their potential
outrage and anger, and yes, their judgment—affect
nearly every word you put on the page. The greatest urge to write is the need to communicate with
that imagined reader, the greatest block is the fear
of rejection. What if I say everything in my heart
and am judged a fool? Or worse, what if they don't
care at all? At candlelight services, at memorials, at
the award ceremony dedicated to Susan's memory,
I could hardly tell if the tears I shed were mine or
theirs or a combination of both. And it frightened me.

I had even waited to begin moving until Darius
was on a trip to visit his grandparents in New Jersey.
I didn't want him to see me as I decided which of
his, his mother's and his brother's belongings would
need to be given away, thrown out or left behind. I
was terrified of him asking me how I could throw
away anything that might hold a memory of his

family, lost in a car accident on another continent. I didn't want to look into the *how could you* eyes of a little boy or coldly look away from them and keep working because I had no answers. He didn't have a gravesite to visit, so why couldn't we keep the winter coat with the holes in it, the stuffed elephant with the stuffing falling out, the three boxes of birthday cards his mother had meticulously packed and stacked for some moment in the future. They were his too. How do you explain to a little boy, honestly, what is happening in your heart and head when you don't understand it yourself?

Susie was an incredible pack rat. Or should I say, a collector of heirlooms, of totems. For her, objects were invested with a certain kind of magic. This is true for all of us to some degree. We keep a baseball glove or a pair of baby shoes hidden away in some trunk in some closet. And for the most part, they remain there. Rarely do any of us return to them, but we fear somehow that throwing away the object would be to eliminate the memory or the moment. Though many garages and closets fill up from laziness, for the most part we just can't find it in us to consign that part of us to a landfill or a recycling bin. But for Susie this impulse to save and collect operated in the mainspring of her personality. Her life was transient and brief and she seemed to sense its brevity, to sense how short her moment was. So she'd hold on to things with an ardor that was nearly desperate. For her, each object had a life, had soul, or perhaps captured a bit of the soul from the hands that touched it, the time it passed through. Objects spoke to her—her grandfather's handkerchief, her first report card, a pair of light blue knit gloves that Cyrus wore as an infant, a stone, a marble, a hairpin.

After ten years of marriage, I had gone from being amused by this eccentricity to being burdened by it. No one could fill up an attic, a basement, a garage or a closet like Susie. As her father's career with the United Nations and then as her own career as an academic took her from one place to another—to New Jersey, to Switzerland, to Texas, to Michigan, to Georgia—she brought everything she could along with her—she even kept the boxes— usually with careful notations regarding what they contained. So if she needed to move again, she could find the exact box and return the object to its temporary home. By the time we had moved into a large A-frame house on Lake Sinclair in Milledgeville,

Georgia, empty boxes filled nearly a third of the garage nearly to the ceiling. If anyone had ever dropped a match, the place would have been in cinders in minutes.

I learned to hate cardboard.

To hate packing. Packing tape. U-Hauls. I didn't mind leaving somewhere. I just couldn't understand the need to take so much of the place along with me. I longed to be disburdened. To be lightened. To be left "with only the shirt on my back" seemed not a curse to me, but a kind of freedom. Of course, up until marrying Susan, my life had been conventional, parochial, and stable. I was a New Englander through to the core and a large transition meant a four-hour drive up the interstate to attend college in Vermont. Most of my journeys were those of the mind. Growing up in a small suburban town to which I felt no particular attachment, the world in which I spent most of my time was imaginary. The American boy in literature, the American spirit in general, is often characterized by wanderlust. Huck Finn setting off on a raft, called away and back again. But I never felt the urge to leave or stay. I was content to sit in one spot for hours, dreaming. My mother still tells people of how she could sit me on the floor of the living room as a baby and I would happily stay there, quietly looking around me, smiling at the world. Of course this turned from a virtue to a problem as I got older and the homework piled up and books were left on busses and report cards came home. My parents would sit me on the couch and plead, threaten, come up with study plans, and I would silently, if ashamedly, stare back from another world, not really understanding why a lost book and an unfinished report mattered so much to everyone when there were so many books to be had, and I was always writing and rewriting them in my head. I was lost in the worlds of the fantasy, science-fiction, and horror novels that I'd read constantly when I was supposed to be doing schoolwork. One time my oldest sister, home from college, and several advanced psychology courses, announced, "I know what it is, Jo Jo has ADD." She then spent a good month trying to convince everyone of the obvious—talking about different medications I could try and different treatments that were available.

But a few years before, a boy from Canton who had been diagnosed with ADHD and placed on Ritalin led a younger child out into the woods and crushed his head with a baseball bat—just because he wanted to know what it would feel like to kill someone. So Lisa's suggestion was treated by everyone as if she had just discovered three sixes carved into the back of my head As a result, I was spared medication and doctor's visits and my faults were attributed to a lack of character and compensated for by hardworking teachers and a growing nervous energy on my part that just may have been caused by hormones. I like to think of myself not as someone with an attention deficit, but as someone with a highly associative mind—one that moves from subject to subject, place to place, with speed and perhaps an awkward, angling grace.

I'm a poet so I understand the power of things, but to me, they remain things—lifeless until animated by memory or emotion—by those who carry, or visit, or use them, to pass back into oblivion when the owner moves on—as they must do. So I move from thing to thing, place to place, as a child skips across the stones on a river. From one state to another, one place to the next.

Moving was much more painful for Susie and her pain became my own. The organization it took was monumental and overwhelming. And still, things got lost. Things got broken and ruined. Each move meant a painful letting go. Each separation injured us and pulled us apart. As I rushed around piling our belongings into crates and onto trucks, she carefully, slowly, maddeningly, turned each object over and over in her hands, before delicately tucking it away. Of course, this is what was most beautiful about her. So much about what you can love about someone is the very thing that can drive you mad with frustration. Susie found the souls of things and would imbibe them with a deep and penetrating spirit. And I have to say, when she touched something, it gained, even to me, the quality of magic. When she'd leave me a note, even a grocery list, I'd stuff it in a pocket, superstitiously afraid to throw out anything on which she written a single line.

* * *

The first house we moved into in Georgia was a small ranch on a hill. It was tiny compared to the large home we had left behind and so quite a bit of our belongings stayed, stacked and packed on wooden tiers in the large, unfinished basement. Still, when I arrived I had to find a way to load a full-sized U-Haul into a two-bedroom ranch home. I managed, but not without making some of the hallways unpassable. The boys were always catching a knee, a shoulder, or—traumatically—their foreheads on the corners of the piano or the washing machine. The carpets, in particular, were a problem. Susan's parents had given her five or six priceless genuine Persian carpets. It was a mystery to me how they managed to get them out of Iran and into the United States, but I always assumed that somehow they had enough of Susan's magic to make little things like customs officers turn the wrong way at the right moment. Those carpets were special to Susan in ways it is hard to communicate. She identified with them. Each had its own intricate and distinctive design. Her favorite was blood red, with gold trim and blue peacocks (at least this is how I remember it, but I have not seen the carpets in some time. They now lie, stacked on top of each other, in the Atefat's home in New Jersey). She would play on them with Cyrus every day, pushing little matchbox cars along the curves of their intricate patterns, as if they were complex highways in some gigantic, wondrous city.

Not long after we "settled" into the home, it seemed to want us out. I know this sounds insane—and Susie and I would laugh about it after we finally did leave for the larger house on the lake. But in the magically charged world surrounding Susan, the idea that houses might be alive and possibly evil was far from absurd. There were red ants and chiggers in the grass and they would chew at the boys' legs and arms, raising large itchy welts that needed to be hosed down and then treated with pink, sticky creams. Mice began to invade, disregarding traps, poison, little noise-makers designed to rattle their tiny brains, and they left their droppings in the kitchen. A train passed once a day and shook the hill our home stood on until decorative plates would tremble and fall from tables. And its sound still follows me in dreams: the hungry, predatory coming on, and then, the ache and emptying of its traveling away. In one dream, Cyrus stares out from the last car, his face as pale and thin as moonlight.

At first, Susan gamely made the best of it all, smiling, making jokes when she could; but I'd catch her at times looking sad, wandering around the place as if she were trying to find a place to sit, but came upon each spot occupied with something wrong and unnamable. Some unhappy ghost. Susan, dark-eyed, raven-haired, and olive-skinned, was as out of place in Milledgeville as her bright red carpets on the floor of that modest little home with the oddly pretentious columns on the front porch. This was not her place and she knew it.

Then came the mold.

One day we noticed that the vents were turning black. So we sprayed them with bleach, only to wake up the following day to see that a dark circle was forming around the grates and traveling out like a cloud.

We stared at it, not speaking, not really knowing what to do.

Before long the mold was traveling up the walls and spreading in the corners, and I found myself washing them daily with a sponge dipped in bleach. Then one morning, Susan lifted a corner of a carpet to move it and found the same dark cloud moving from the corner in, directly to its peacock heart. I can't remember exactly, but I think she screamed. What I do remember is the expression on her face, pale, mouth open, her eyes drawn together in a disbelieving stare. She looked exactly as I might imagine someone might after just being told she had cancer and possibly, months to live.

Right around that time, Susan developed a high fever and pain that radiated around her eyes, and I couldn't help but wonder if the mold in the carpet's fiber was eating her away as well. *Its just the flu,* I told myself but the fever grew and grew, until one day I heard a thud behind me, as if someone had dropped a bag of sand on the floor. I looked over and there was Susan, wrapped in a blanket, covered in sweat, and barely conscious.

"It's a sinus infection," said the young, rather ambivalent emergency room doctor at the local hospital. "A really severe sinus infection."

We started looking for a new place that weekend, deciding that the mold spores had probably caused the illness. But as I loaded our lives back into their designated containers for yet another trip, I found myself more careful than ever. *Step on a crack, break your mother's back* sing the little children hopping along the sidewalks back from school. For them the world is made of such strong and strange dark magic—the radiance of things. Everyone's picture is Dorian Gray's.

I learned to fear the magic of things.

I still don't really know what to do with Susie's and Cyrus's belongings. Our things. And my letting go has been painfully gradual. It has been four years since she died and I've moved three times since then.

Ten miles up the road from the house I rent, just off the business loop on Ohio 32, her piano sits in Bob's Storage along with her tenure review folders and tiffany lamps, and, of course, the box of Cyrus's elementary school art. For years, I kept even the house we lived in (she couldn't or wouldn't sell it after we got different jobs in a different state), faithfully paying the difference between the rent and the mortgage—just barely staying out of debt, determined to keep this one thing—until the tenants left and I had to ask her parents to buy me out. *It wasn't really my home anyway*, I tried to tell myself. We were all co-owners. Her father put up the down payment after all. And he wasn't going to sell it. So I let it go, signing documents, taking on the taxes, trying to catch my breath, telling myself that the house, too, was just a thing.

But things—objects, photographs, a lost glove, a baby's stocking—have a way of coming back and haunting us.

About a year ago, just after I had finally unpacked the last box, stacked the last dish, finally set up Darius's new room with a new bed and Spongebob decals on the wall, Susan's mother called, desperate:

Joel, I must talk with you. I'm going crazy. The basement, Joel. The basement.

I knew instinctively what had happened. The house was an old one and it was serviced by two water sources—town water for drinking, and well water from a pump in the basement for watering the lawn. Before winter, every year, I'd have to drain the outside lines and turn off the pump or the old pipes would freeze and crack. I had assumed the Atefats, who had spent so many months living with us, knew everything there was to know about running the house. But they weren't actually living there. And they weren't renting it either. It sat unoccupied, a giant cardboard box, filled up with ghosts.

So much was lost. She kept everything. I remember you used to make a joke of it, saying you were surprised she flushed the toilet, but for us it is no joke.

Did I really say that? Yes, I did. Sometimes I was such a bastard. And I imagine I said much worse. As Susan's mother told me about the childhood schoolwork and baby clothes (Susie had kept almost everything Cyrus wore that first year), the winter parkas, the dolls, the notebooks she had carefully laid out to dry in the garage, I thought of how resentment builds and piles up, word by harsh or poorly chosen word. How we store these things in piles, unable to let go, and carry them around until they bend or break our backs beneath their weight.

I tried to say something honest and hopeful:

But you know, Cyrus and Susie are not in those things. They are beyond them.

You don't understand. You've let go but it is much harder for us. This is all we have of them.

I could hear her gasp for air between the words. I wanted to say so much more. How those things on the driveway were empty from the start. How their daughter and grandson, thrown into eternity on the desert highway in Jordan, weren't contained by things any more than a temple or a church can hold God. But by then I was crying too—silently.

You don't understand. You've let go.

Not yet. But I'm trying.

Four years, and three homes. I've even remarried, but still I am letting go, piece by piece.

* * *

Everything is metaphor. Everything symbolic. Each box another memory, another dream—the ones I save, the ones I store, the ones I open on occasion and weep over, only to close again, sealed with clear packing tape.

In moments of brutal honesty and clarity I know that "letting go" is as much about my fear of facing the past as it is about accepting the future. The pull of an object can be tidal when lit by memory. And I fear spending my life split between times—by a love-note falling from an old book, or by something as simple as a grocery list found in the pocket of suit I haven't worn in years.

So I don't just let go: I misplace, forget, lose, and neglect. Though I pay seventy dollars a month for storage, I've "forgotten" the combination to the gate and "lost" the keys to the lock. Even that bike left outside from season to season—did a part of me hope I would come home from work one evening to find it gone, peddled away by some blessed little thief?

* * *

If it weren't for Susan's mother, the bike would never have made it to New Hampshire. I don't clearly remember making a decision about it. We had returned to Georgia a few months after the accident to clear out the house. Still heavily medicated and in shock, I floated among the furniture. Nearly every-thing was as we had left it. The Atefats had taken the carpets and the furniture they had given us (with my blessings), but everything else remained. Even a few of the toys—a stuffed elephant, a stray match-box car—lay on the floor as if the owner had simply gotten up to go the bathroom in the middle of play. I remember breaking down and almost falling on my crutches. I remember sobbing in a way that scared me. I remember my mother-in-law holding me as I wept. We stood there, bathed in sunlight coming off the lake and through the glass porch doors. And I swear the house trembled around us.

I remember how my shoulders went limp into her arms before I really knew who was holding me. I felt vulnerable and exposed there in the light. I felt as if I could do anything. I don't know if my parents watched but imagined they must have, standing there, staring at the two of us, not know-ing what to do or say—just wanting to pull me out of that moment, away from that grief, and push me forward into life. And I don't remember what happened next—when I stopped crying or after how long. I only wanted out of that embrace—that attempt to share what was and could only be mine in that moment. To be alone. Just alone in that house. To be shattered to dust by light. I imagined myself as some B-movie vampire standing near an open window as the sun pours in on him, his skin turning to ash.

I didn't turn to ash. Instead, I spent three days trying to breathe as my parents and sister and brother-in-law worked feverishly to empty and clean that home of any sign we had ever lived there. We couldn't take everything. The rented dumpster on the lawn filled and overflowed, several truckloads of clothing and toys went to the salvation army bins, to recycling bins. The Atefats played goalie, frantically trying to save anything of significance. Ugly things were said from under the breath and over angry sighs as doors closed and feet came up and down the steps. The Atefats would coax and cajole Darius:

You want this, don't you? Don't you want to wear something of your brother's when you get to be a big boy?

Strangely, he would mostly say no.

No; I said no. I don't want it—and then retreat to the water's edge where he would take his little Mickey Mouse fishing rod and practice casting the little rubber weight out into Lake Sinclair as my brother-in-law Jeff gave him pointers, told silly jokes. I watched them from the sun room as I went through Susan's desk, making a pile of what I would keep and what I would let go of. I had never gone through Susie's desk before, and I felt the terrible violation of it. I couldn't even find the key to the top drawer and had to break into it with a knife. When it finally popped open, I found ten years of Valentine's Day cards. I remember scanning the words, some in my haphazard scrawl, some penned beautifully in her almost obsessively careful script, stopping on the ones that stung. I looked up at my father, his hair tousled with work, his searching and sad eyes

—*What do I do with these?*

And honestly, I don't know if they sit in a box somewhere or if I threw them away. I know I've never looked for them again.

But many things survived that day and followed me. Some still do.

When I slid open the storage container behind the Wal-Mart in West Lebanon, New Hampshire, it was like opening the door to a child's untidy closet. Objects tumbled out—as if they were alive and desperate for light and air. Stray Spongebob and Scooby-Doo, t-shirts fell onto the ground, a light blue ball rolled to my feet, and there, sitting in front of a piano left tipped on it side, was the bike, Cyrus's bike.

For some reason, though I had no plans to retrieve anything that day, I threw the bike and a couple of loose toys into the car and drove it up the hill to my little dormitory apartment. By this time, Darius had his own big-boy bike—a slick, metallic blue one, and soon he would have no need for training wheels. But his brother's little red huffy sat at the front of the steps like a sentinel through our first fall on the mountain, and then the snows of winter. Untouched, it rusted in the elements, and with one training wheel slightly raised off the uneven ground, it looked for all the world as if some little boy would return after school, hop on it and ride dangerously out onto the road, risking death, the ways boys do. And he would grow and I'd take off the trainers and bring him to a track or an empty parking lot and run behind him as he laughed with delight, until I let go of the seat and watched him wobble and straighten, losing and gaining control, nearly falling and righting himself again, like some small boat on a high sea. And I'd feel that tender pull a parent feels at the first stirring of a child's freedom—that longing to let him go and have him back again. *Don't grow up so fast little man. We have so much to do.*

* * *

We will never have that day. Letting go of the past is not really the problem. The boxes aren't the problem. I could sit happily in memory forever, and I would keep your things for you, your mother's too, if all they held were memory. If their magic did not include the glimmer of a future that is gone. But the mind will not stay still. I leap from "now" into "if only" far too easily. And then I am lost in the woods. It is the future we hold fast to, that we cannot give up without a ripping pain in solar plexus and the gut.

* * *

I waited until nightfall to throw out the bike. I would do this thing alone without any eyes to judge or capture it. I would lift it above my head with only a few faint stars as witness. I would let go and it would be gone like so much was gone and I would be free. I remember the sweat beginning to chill on my back in the night air and how light and fragile

the bike felt in my hands. I stood there for a long
time. And then I threw it into the air, into the darkness. I don't remember the sound of it hitting the
inside of the dumpster. There was a roar in my head,
I think—blood maybe, or the wind kicking up, or a
train hurtling through the dark.